Editiones Roche

The Cost of Life
Paddy Hartley

Basel

Texte von
Jonathan
Steffen

Texts by
Jonathan
Steffen

13. September 2021–
23. Januar 2022

September 13, 2021–
January 23, 2022

Basel

Berwick

Basel

Einleitung

Roche hat im Lauf ihrer 125jährigen Geschichte die meisten Jubiläen auch mit der Beauftragung von Kunstwerken festgehalten. 1921 fiel der 25. Geburtstag der Gründung des Unternehmens jedoch in eine Zeit der Krise, so wurde dieser kaum gefeiert. Dies holte man erst 1936 anlässlich der Eröffnung des Verwaltungsgebäudes in Basel nach. Als 40jähriges Jubiläum ist es das Einzige, welches den üblichen 25-Jahres-Rhythmus durchbrach, gleichzeitig wurde erstmals ein Kunstwerk in Auftrag gegeben. Das 6 mal 6 Meter messende Wandbild von Niklaus Stoecklin, nach einem Wettbewerb entstanden, gilt auch als Beginn der Kunstsammlung des Unternehmens. Zum 100. Geburtstag 1996 schenkte Roche der Stadt Basel und damit auch sich selbst das Museum Tinguely, welches bis heute unser bedeutendstes Engagement in der Förderung bildender Kunst darstellt.

Seither hat sich die Beziehung der Pharmaindustrie zur Gesellschaft enorm gewandelt. Das zentrale Anliegen von Roche ist die Kommunikation mit den Patienten — ein Anliegen, das heute in der Mitte der Gesellschaft angekommen ist. Roche ist eine Verfechterin des offenen Diskurses über die umstrittenen Sachverhalte im Gesundheitswesen und hat — seit der öffentlichen Veranstaltungsreihe «Roche informiert», die ab 1987 in der Messe Basel stattfand — die transparente Kommunikation über umstrittene Themen kontinuierlich ausgebaut und gepflegt. In vielerlei Hinsicht startete dieser Prozess mit dem Symposium «The Challenge of Life — Biomedical Progress and Human Values», welches zum 75jährigen Jubiläum 1971 mit hochkarätiger internationaler Beteiligung von Roche ausgerichtet worden ist. Nebst vielen anderen Erkenntnissen zeigte diese Veranstaltung vor allem die Diskrepanzen in der gegenseitigen Wahrnehmung der verschiedenen Anspruchsgruppen und auch von Roche selbst auf, die es durch Dialog zu überbrücken galt und gilt.

Es lag für uns nahe, einen Bezug zu den Erkenntnissen des Symposiums «The Challenge of Life zu schaffen, welches eng mit unserem 125. Geburtstag verknüpft ist. Dieser wird unter dem Motto «Celebrate Life» gefeiert, und um ihn angemessen zu begehen, haben wir den Britischen Künstler Paddy Hartley mit einer Werkgruppe beauftragt, die aktuelle Anliegen der Patientenerfahrung im Licht der Veränderungen seit 1971 darstellt. Die Ausstellung «The Cost of Life» — der Titel wurde von Paddy Hartley selbst gewählt — ist einmaliger künstlerischer Ausdruck dessen, was uns als Unternehmen heute zutiefst beschäftigt.

Wir hoffen, dass der Blick des Künstlers auf diese Themen viele Besucherinnen und Besucher der Ausstellung dazu anregt, offen über die tiefgreifenden und innigen Beziehungen zwischen der Gesellschaft, dem Gesundheitswesen und der Pharmaindustrie nachzudenken. Für Paddy Hartley steht die Erfahrung der Patienten im Mittelpunkt seines Werks. Auch wir bei Roche stellen das Schicksal der Patienten in den Mittelpunkt unserer Anstrengungen. Wir befassen uns mit schwierigen und oftmals belastenden Themen, dies kommt in «The Cost of Life» zum Ausdruck. Oftmals erkennen wir erst im Rückblick, wie bahnbrechend viele Fortschritte in der Behandlung und Therapie von Krankheiten waren. Auch dies wird in Paddy Hartleys Ausstellung reflektiert. Unser Bekenntnis, diesen Fortschritt voranzutreiben, ist der wichtigste Beitrag, den Roche der Menschheit zu leisten imstande ist. Wir führen unsere Unterstützung für originäre Kunst und originelles Denken beständig fort.

Dr. Christoph Franz
Präsident des Verwaltungsrats
Roche Holding AG

Basel

Berwick

Basel

Introduction

During the course of its 125-year history, Roche has commissioned original art to help mark the majority of its jubilees. The 25th anniversary of the company's founding fell in 1921, at a time of existential crisis for Roche, and consequently went almost without celebration. This omission was rectified in 1936, however, on the occasion of the opening of the head office building in Basel. This 40-year jubilee was the only one that broke with the usual 25-year cycle. It was also the first to involve the commissioning of a work of art, in the form of a mural by Niklaus Stoecklin. The product of an invitational competition, this work — measuring a full 6 metres square — is today considered the nucleus of the company's art collection. Sixty years later, on the occasion of its centenary in 1996, Roche presented the city of Basel, and therefore also itself, with the Museum Tinguely, which immediately became the company's pre-eminent cultural commitment in the fine arts.

Since then, the relationship between the pharmaceutical industry and society at large has undergone a fundamental transformation. Today, Roche's prime concern is communication with patients — a concern that has grown to occupy a central position within society as a whole. Roche advocates open discussion of controversial issues in healthcare and has encouraged transparent communication in this area ever since staging the milestone public information event 'Roche informs' held from 1987 at the Basel Fair. In many respects, this encouragement of open discussion was initiated by the symposium 'The Challenge of Life — Biomedical Progress and Human Values', which the company hosted to mark its 75th anniversary in 1971, and which featured a roster of internationally renowned speakers. Besides its many other outcomes, this event served to highlight the differences in the mutual perceptions of the various stakeholders, including Roche itself. These could only be addressed through dialogue — an endeavour that continues to this day.

Distant though they may seem now, the insights that sprang from 'The Challenge of Life' symposium are highly pertinent to the celebration of our company's 125th anniversary. It is held under the motto 'Celebrate Life' and to help celebrate this milestone, we commissioned the British artist Paddy Hartley to create a suite of artworks that explore contemporary concerns about the patient experience in the light of the changes that have occurred since 1971. 'The Cost of Life' exhibition — a title chosen by Paddy Hartley himself — is a unique artistic statement that explores our deepest concerns as a company today.

We hope that Paddy Hartley's perspective on the issues addressed in this exhibition will encourage visitors to reflect on the profound and intimate relationships between society, healthcare and the pharmaceutical industry. The experience of the patient is central to Paddy Hartley's work. It is likewise the focus of Roche's endeavours. This experience — often complex, sometimes painful, always challenging — is what 'The Cost of Life' explores. Often it is only with hindsight that we fully understand the full significance of advances that have been achieved in the prevention and treatment of injury and disease. This understanding is reflected in Paddy Hartley's exhibition. Our commitment to continuing those advances is the most important contribution that we as a company can make to humankind. Our support for original art, and for original thinking, continues.

Dr. Christoph Franz
Chairman of the Board of Directors
Roche Holding Ltd.

Ein einzigartiger Blickwinkel: «The Cost of Life»

Anlässlich des 125. Jubiläums von Roche

Im Oktober 2021 feiert das Unternehmen Hoffmann-La Roche das 125. Jubiläum seiner Gründung in der Schweizer Grenzstadt Basel. Um dieses Ereignis würdig zu begehen, richtet Roche eine einzigartige Ausstellung zum Thema «The Cost of Life» aus. Der eine Teil dieser Ausstellung im Museum Tinguely in Basel umfasst eine Serie neuer keramischer Kunstwerke des Britischen Künstlers Paddy Hartley. Separat dazu richtet der Künstler eine Intervention im Pharmaziemuseum der Universität Basel ein. Beide Ausstellungen finden von Anfang Oktober 2021 bis Ende Januar 2022 statt. Zusammen spüren sie — vor dem Hintergrund der wissenschaftlichen und medizinischen Entwicklungen der letzten fünfzig Jahre — der Wahrnehmung und den Erfahrungen von heutigen Patientinnen und Patienten nach.

Zu der Vision des Unternehmens bezüglich «The Cost of Life» befragt, stellt Alexander Bieri, Kurator des Historischen Archivs von Roche, fest: «Roche hat das Ziel, medizinische Lösungen zu erforschen, herzustellen und weltweit zu vertreiben. Dieser Unternehmenszweck hat sich in 125 Jahren nie verändert, obwohl sich Roche kontinuierlich neu erfunden hat, um neuartige Technologien zur Behandlung von Krankheiten auf den Markt zu bringen. Ich hoffe, dass diese beiden Ausstellungen die Besucherinnen und Besucher dazu anregen werden, sich Fragen zu der Beziehung zwischen Patienten und den medizinischen Wissenschaften im weitesten Sinn zu stellen. Diese Beziehung ist komplex und herausfordernd. Als pharmazeutisches Unternehmen zeigen wir mit diesen beiden Ausstellungen, dass wir unsere Geschichte so akzeptieren, wie sie sich zugetragen hat und dass wir gegenüber unserer Tätigkeit ehrlich und offen sind: Weswegen wir unserem Unternehmenszweck nachgehen, wie wir dies tun und was dies für Einzelne und die Gesellschaft als Ganzes bedeutet.»

ROCHE WAR VON ANBEGINN auf wissenschaftliche Forschung ausgerichtet. Labor bei Roche Grenzach, Forschungschef Markus Guggenheim, 1911.

ROCHE FOCUSED from the beginning on scientific research. Laboratory in Roche Grenzach, head of research Markus Guggenheim, 1911.

Als Pharmaunternehmen zeigen wir, dass wir gegenüber unserer Tätigkeit ehrlich und offen sind.

Roche marks its 125th Anniversary

A Unique View of 'The Cost of Life'

In October 2021, the company of Hoffmann-La Roche celebrates the 125th Anniversary of its founding in Basel, Switzerland. To mark this milestone, the company has commissioned a unique exhibition on the theme 'The Cost of Life'. The exhibition, staged at the Museum Tinguely in Basel, comprises a suite of original new ceramic artworks by the British artist Paddy Hartley. It is accompanied by a separate intervention at the Pharmacy Museum of the University of Basel. These two exhibitions run from the start of October 2021 till the end of January 2022. Taken together, they explore the perceptions and experiences of patients today against the background of the scientific and medical developments of the past half-century.

Reflecting on the company's vision for 'The Cost of Life', Alexander Bieri, Curator of the Roche Historical Collection and Archive, observes: "Roche exists to research and manufacture drugs and to market them globally. The company's purpose has not changed in 125 years, although Roche has reinvented itself time and again as it has explored new technologies in search of solutions to unmet medical needs. I hope that these two events will stimulate visitors to ask themselves questions about the relationship between the patient and medical science in the widest sense. It is a relationship that is complex and challenging. By staging these two exhibitions, we are showing as a pharmaceutical company that we accept our history as it is and are honest and open about what we do, why we do it, how we do it, and what this can mean for individuals and for society as a whole."

ALS GLOBALES UNTERNEHMEN in drei Ländern gleichzeitig gegründet, war Grenzach in Deutschland lange Zeit der wichtigste Standort. Flugaufnahme um 1920.

FOUNDED AS A GLOBAL COMPANY simultaneously in three countries, Grenzach in Germany remained the most important site for long time. Aerial view, c. 1920.

We are showing as a pharma company that we are honest and open about what we do.

FRITZ HOFFMANN-LA ROCHE, Gründer von Roche und Pionier der pharmazeutischen Industrie, um 1910.

FRITZ HOFFMANN-LA ROCHE, founder of Roche and pioneer of the pharmaceutical industry, c. 1910.

Ungelöste medizinische Herausforderungen anpacken

Die F. Hoffmann-La Roche & Co. wurde am 1. Oktober 1896 durch den Schweizer Unternehmer Fritz Hoffmann-La Roche als Nachfolgefirma der Hoffmann-Traub & Co. gegründet. Fritz Hoffmann-La Roche hatte wenige Jahre zuvor die Cholera-Epidemie von 1892 in Hamburg (Deutschland) selbst miterlebt. Diese Erfahrung half, seine Überzeugung zu festigen, dass Krankheiten auf breiter Front bekämpft werden könnten, indem wissenschaftliche Forschungsergebnisse zur Erzeugung standardisierter Medikamente in industriellem Massstab herbeigezogen würden. Dieses Ziel wurde zu seinem Lebensinhalt; als er Hoffmann-La Roche gründete, war er gerade einmal 28 Jahre alt. Roche wurde als Reaktion auf ein medizinisches Problem gegründet und ist einzigartig, weil das Unternehmen zu diesem Zeitpunkt weder über ein Produkt noch über eine Technologie, die dafür hätte eingesetzt werden können, verfügte. Die Vorgängerfirma war nämlich vorwiegend in der Herstellung von Seife und Bohnerwachs, neben anderen Drogerieprodukten, engagiert.

Es war Fritz Hoffmann-La Roche, der diese Firma nach der Übernahme auf einen völlig neuen Zweck ausrichtete. Dies tat er mit Kapital seiner Familie und von Freunden, was ihm grosse Unabhängigkeit gewährte. Die junge Firma konnte somit sehr früh mit neuen Technologien experimentieren, ohne durch eine diesbezügliche Tradition belastet zu sein: Mit der Entwicklung des ersten Prozesses zur Herstellung synthetischer Ascorbinsäure (Vitamin C) begann bereits in den 1930er Jahren die Ära der mikrobiologischen Wirkstoffproduktion. Schon in den 1960er Jahren begann Roche, Diagnostika herzustellen und startete ein Programm zur Entwicklung von Geräten. Die Tatsache, dass Roche im Gegensatz zu vielen anderen Unternehmen in der Lage war, sich kontinuierlich neu zu erfinden, ist auf die Unabhängigkeit von einer bestimmten Technologie zurückzuführen. Dies trifft auch heute noch zu: Roche entwickelt sich in Reaktion auf ungelöste medizinische Bedürfnisse. Nach 125 Jahren immer noch dem Grundsatz verpflichtet zu sein, medizinische Herausforderungen zu meistern, ist eine bemerkenswerte Leistung.

Das Symposium «The Challenge of Life»

Vom 31. August bis zum 3. September 1971 führte Roche ein Symposium in Basel durch, dessen Titel «The Challenge of Life: Biomedical Progress and Human Values» lautete. Ein Auszug aus dem Tagungsprotokoll erklärt, worum es hier ging: «*Während der 75 Jahre des Bestehens von Roche hat sich die Forschung bei weitem zu der grössten Abteilung innerhalb des Unternehmens entwickelt. Zunehmend spielt die Grundlagenforschung eine wichtige Rolle darin; aus diesem Grund fühlt Roche eine Mitverantwortung für die vielen Probleme, welche der biomedizinische Fortschritt aufwirft. Somit entstand die Idee, den Geburtstag nicht in üblicher Weise zu feiern und Roche stattdessen bei der Arbeit zu zeigen. Sicherlich eine besondere Art der Arbeit, nicht die tägliche Routine, sondern eine Sphäre der freien Kommunikation mit Intellektuellen, die von ausserhalb des Einflussbereichs der üblichen Tätigkeiten des Unternehmens stammen. So wurde die Idee einer multidisziplinären Tagung geboren, die sich mit einem Thema befassen soll, welches eine Debatte über die wissenschaftlichen Zielsetzungen des Unternehmens und ihrer Beziehung zur Gesellschaft auslöst: Die humanen Probleme des biomedizinischen Fortschritts.*»

Das Symposium «The Challenge of Life» war ein wichtiger Wendepunkt in der Lebensspanne des Unternehmens: Es forderte Roche selbst heraus und veränderte den Kurs der Firma für die kommenden Jahrzehnte. Die Feierlichkeiten zum 125. Geburtstag sind absichtlich an diejenigen des 75. Jubiläums angelehnt, aber der Fokus hat sich von «The Challenge of Life» zu «The Cost of Life» verändert.

Roche ist einzigartig, weil sie als Reaktion auf ein medizinisches Problem gegründet wurde

DAS ERSTE GEBÄUDE, welches Fritz Hoffmann-La Roche für das junge Unternehmen errichten liess. Verwaltungsbau 1, Basel, 1905.

THE FIRST BUILDING which was erected by Fritz Hoffmann-La Roche for the fledgling company. Administration building 1, Basel, 1905.

Tackling unsolved medical challenges

F. Hoffmann-La Roche & Co. was founded in Basel, Switzerland on 1 October 1896 by the Swiss entrepreneur Fritz Hoffmann-La Roche as the successor company to Hoffmann, Traub & Co. Fritz Hoffmann-La Roche had had experience of the devastation wrought by the 1892 cholera epidemic in Hamburg, Germany. This experience helped shape his belief that disease might be tackled on a large scale by the research and industrial manufacture of medicines based on standardised compounds. It was this objective to which he dedicated most of his working life; he had been only 28 when he founded Hoffmann-La Roche. The company of Roche is therefore unique because it was founded in response to a medical problem, although it did not possess either a product or a technology that specifically addressed that problem at the time of its founding. In fact, the predecessor company had been a manufacturer of soap and floor polish amongst other things.

Fritz Hoffmann-La Roche took that company and adapted it to serve completely new purposes, supported only by such funds as he could supply, backed up by the resources of some of his friends. This state of affairs offered him great independence, and it gave the new company freedom to venture into new technologies at a very early stage: molecular biology in the 1930s, for instance, with the development of the first process for the synthesis and industrial manufacture of vitamin C, or again, diagnostics in the 1960s. One thing that was distinct about Roche was that it was capable of reinventing itself time and again because it was not dependent of a particular technology. That remains true today: Roche evolves in response to unmet medical needs. To have survived for 125 years, and still to be tackling unsolved medical challenges, is a remarkable achievement.

The 'Challenge of Life' Symposium

From 31 August to 3 September 1971, Roche held a symposium in Basel whose title was 'The Challenge of Life: Biomedical Progress and Human Values.' To quote from the symposium proceedings: "*During the 75 years of Roche the research division has become by far the largest department in the company, with basic research assuming an increasingly important part in it. For this reason Roche cannot but feel a share of the responsibility towards the many problems raised by biomedical progress. Hence, the idea of celebrating the anniversary along conventional lines could not be seriously entertained. The occasion was to show Roche at work. A special kind of work certainly, breaking away from the daily routine into the sphere of free communication with thinking people outside the purview of the company's usual tasks. Thus was born the idea of a multidisciplinary symposium with a subject which would throw open to discussion the scientific endeavours of the company in their relation to society — the human problems of biomedical progress.*"

'The Challenge of Life' was a significant watershed in the life of the company: it challenged Roche itself and reset the company's course for decades to come. The company's 125th Anniversary celebrations deliberately reference those of the 75th, but the focus has moved on from 'The Challenge of Life' to 'The Cost of Life'.

Roche is unique because it was founded in response to a medical problem

ANLÄSSLICH DES 75jährigen Jubiläums von Roche organisierte das Unternehmen das hochkarätig besetzte Symposium «The Challenge of Life». Es galt, den als sich vertiefend wahrgenommenen Graben zwischen der Allgemeinheit und der Wissenschaft zu überbrücken und eine Übersicht über die sich verändernden ethischen Werte zu gewinnen. Für Roche wurden die Ergebnisse richtungsweisend.

ON THE OCCASION of Roche's 75 year jubilee, the company organised the symposium «The Challenge of Life» and invited illustrious guests to attend. The aim was to bridge the gap between the general public and science, perceived as widening at the time and to gain an overview of the changing ethical values in society. The results pointed the way ahead for Roche.

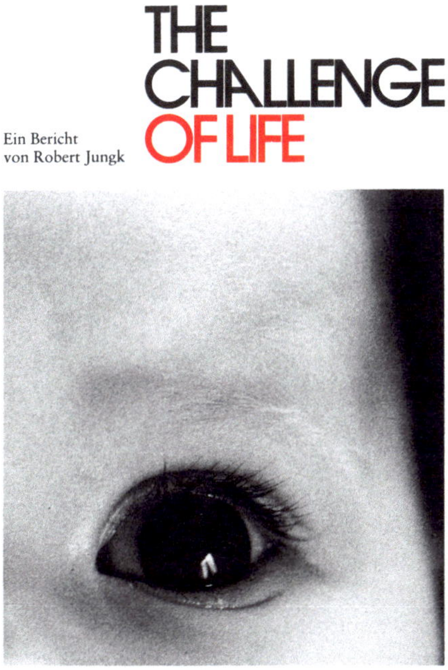

DAS SYMPOSIUM «The Challenge of Life» 1971 erörterte kritische Fragen rund um den biomedizinischen Fortschritt und der ethischen Aspekte wissenschaftlicher Forschung. Eingeladen waren Persönlichkeiten wie Margaret Mead, Philip Handler und Niels Jerne (Bilder oben und oben Mitte). Robert Jungk verfasste aus den Tagungsaufzeichnungen ein populäres Taschenbuch, das die Debatten einem breiten Publikum nahe brachte.

THE SYMPOSIUM 'The Challenge of Life' 1971 discussed critical issues around biomedical progress and ethical aspects of scientific research. The illustrious roster included Margaret Mead, Philip Handler and Niels Jerne (pictured above and above middle). From the proceedings, Robert Jungk created a paperback issue which brought the debates to the attention of the general public.

BEREITS IM Jahr 1936 erwarb Roche das erste Kunstwerk. Niklaus Stoecklins Arzneipflanzenbild bezeugt Roches Ursprung als frühes Pharmaunternehmen.

ALREADY IN 1936 Roche acquired its first artwork. Niklaus Stoecklin's mural with medical plants bears testimony to Roche's origin as an early pharmaceutical enterprise.

Dialog zwischen der Forschung und der breiten Öffentlichkeit stimulieren

Inspiriert durch die Überzeugung bei Roche, dass Kunst dann nützlich ist, wenn sie ihr Publikum herausfordert, stellt dieses Projekt ein Kernelement des laufenden Dialogs zwischen der Wissenschaft und der breiten Öffentlichkeit dar. Im Mittelpunkt stehen die Fragen zu Zweck und Ethik pharmazeutischer Forschung und Produktion. Die Absicht von «The Cost of Life» ist aufzuzeigen, dass Roche offen über ihre Produkte, Behandlungskonzepte und Medikamente reflektiert, indem diese Themen über eine Ausstellung mit Kunstwerken aufgegriffen und zur Diskussion gestellt werden. Diese Themen beinhalten beispielsweise die Verlängerung von Leben, Gentechnologie, das Recht, den eigenen Todeszeitpunkt zu bestimmen, Palliativmedizin, Forschung als Verheissung oder Gefahr für die Menschheit und die Modifikation des Körpers.

Der hauptsächliche Fokus der Ausstellung liegt bei drei Aspekten: Der Beginn des Lebens, das Ende des Lebens und die Herausforderung, die Qualität des Lebens zu steigern anstelle das Leben einfach zu verlängern («adding life to years rather than years to life»), ein fundamentaler Grundsatz der Philosophie von Roche als Pharmaunternehmen. Durch die Beauftragung der Ausstellung «The Cost of Life» vertieft Roche ihr langjähriges Engagement in den bildenden Künsten. Das Projekt «The Cost of Life» strebt zusätzlich an, die Reputation des Unternehmens als verantwortlicher Partner der Gesellschaft zu erhöhen und die Verbindung zu und zwischen lokalen und globalen Interessensgruppen im Bereich der Künste und der Wissenschaften zu vertiefen.

Die Wahl von Paddy Hartley

Seit langer Zeit ist Roche daran interessiert, mit Kunstschaffenden zusammenzuarbeiten, die sich mit der Sichtweise von Patientinnen und Patienten auseinandersetzen. Diese Beschreibung passt perfekt zu Paddy Hartley. Während es viele Künstlerinnen und Künstler gibt, die sich für die Beziehung zwischen Wissenschaft und Kunst interessieren, ist Paddys Interessensgebiet deutlich weiter gefasst. Er setzt sich mit der Erfahrung der Patienten auseinander, beispielsweise mit der Empfindung von Schmerz, und er hat eine einzigartige Art gefunden, dies über eine philosophische Sichtweise auszudrücken. Dieser patientenzentrierte Blickwinkel und Paddys Bemühen, das Patientenschicksal zu artikulieren, fällt vollständig mit der patientenorientierten Philosophie von Roche zusammen.

Roche war über das Projekt «Façade» auf den Künstler aufmerksam geworden, eine bahnbrechende Ausstellung, die chirurgische, soziale und militärgeschichtliche Elemente umfasste. Paddy führte diese am King's College London (KCL) durch und arbeitete dafür eng mit Dr. Ian Thompson (KCL), Dr. Andrew Bamji (ehemaliger Kurator des Gillies Archive), William Edwards (Kurator des Gordon Museum of Anatomy, KCL) und Professor Malcolm Logan von der Randall Division of Cell and Molecular Biophysics (KCL) zusammen.

Dieses Projekt brachte einem internationalen Publikum erstmals die bislang unbekannten Geschichten der Veteranen des Ersten Weltkriegs und derer verheerender Gesichtsverletzungen, die sie im Kampf erlitten hatten, zur Kenntnis. Paddy Hartley möchte mit «The Cost of Life» den Blickwinkel auf drei primäre Themengebiete erweitern, die beinhalten, wie die biomedizinischen Wissenschaften die Gesellschaft und das Individuum beeinflussen und welche die Gesamtheit der menschlichen Lebensspanne von der Geburt bis zum Tod umfassen. Diese sind Embryologie und das Recht, Leben zu erschaffen; die Ursachen und Konsequenzen altersbedingter Erkrankungen; sowie die Euthanasie und das Recht, den Umfang medizinischer Behandlung am Lebensende selbst zu bestimmen.

Adding life to years rather than years to life

Stimulating dialogue between science and the public at large

Inspired by Roche's belief that art needs to challenge people in order to be useful, this project is a core element in the ongoing dialogue between science and the public at large about the purpose and ethics of pharmaceutical research and manufacture. The purpose of the 'Cost of Life' exhibition is to demonstrate Roche's willingness to reflect openly on its products, treatments and medicines by putting these topics up for discussion via an exhibition of original artworks. These topics include, for example, the prolongation of life, genetic engineering, the right to die, palliative care, research as a promise or threat to humanity, and body modification.

The main focus of the exhibition is on three aspects: the beginning of life, the end of life, and the challenge of adding life to years rather than years to life, which is fundamental to the philosophy of Roche as a pharmaceutical company. By commissioning 'The Cost of Life', Roche further emphasises its continuing role as a significant patron of the arts. 'The Cost of Life' project aims additionally to increase the company's reputation as a responsible partner to society and to intensify its connection to local and global communities interested in the arts, the sciences, and the relationships between them.

FÜR DAS von Roche gegründete «Basel Institute for Immunology» schuf Jean Tinguely (rechts) 1971 die Arbeit «Doppelhelix».

FOR THE «Basel Institute for Immunology» which was founded by Roche, Jean Tinguely (right) created the artwork «Double Helix» in 1971.

The selection of Paddy Hartley

Roche was interested in commissioning original work from an artist who had a patient-centred view — a description that perfectly fits Paddy Hartley. There are many artists who are interested in the relationship between art and science, but Paddy's interest goes much further than that. He is interested in the experience of the patient, in the experience of pain, and he has a unique way of expressing this from a philosophical viewpoint. This patient-centred view and Paddy's commitment to articulating 'the patient's plight' aligns fully with Roche's patient-centric philosophy.

Roche was familiar with 'Project Façade', a landmark exhibition combining elements of surgical, social and military history that Paddy carried out at King's College London (KCL) in close collaboration with Dr Ian Thompson of KCL, Dr Andrew Bamji formerly Gillies Archive Curator, William Edwards, Curator of the Gordon Museum (KCL) and Professor Malcolm Logan at the Randall Division of Cell and Molecular Biophysics (KCL).

That project brought to the attention of an international audience the untold histories of First World War servicemen treated for the horrific facial injuries they had sustained in action. In 'The Cost of Life' project, Paddy Hartley widens his focus to cover three primary subject areas that concern how biomedical science influences society and the individual and cover the totality of the human lifespan, from birth to death. These are: embryology and the right to create life; the causes and consequences of age-related disease; and euthanasia and the right to facilitate elective end-of-life treatment.

Adding life to years rather than years to life

Ein Vierteljahrhundert der Auseinandersetzung

Für «The Cost of Life» hat Paddy die Entscheidung getroffen, hauptsächlich Porzellanpapier in weissen und roten Glasuren zu verwenden, wobei er zusätzlich Metall, Glas und Textilien einsetzt, wo dies angebracht erscheint. Die Kunstwerke sind unterschiedlichen Formats, jedoch durchgängig auf Sockeln ausgestellt. Die Inspiration dazu entstammt den Gesprächen, die Paddy während 25 Jahren mit Patienten und Medizinern geführt hat, die über intime Kenntnis der drei ausgesuchten Themen verfügen.

Diese fundierten Einsichten werden durch Paddys eigene Erfahrungen ergänzt. Die Kunstwerke artikulieren seine Überlegungen zu den von ihm geführten Gesprächen und sie referenzieren sich gegenseitig, sodass die Themen des einen Werks in anderer Form in einem oder mehreren der anderen Werke auftauchen. So stellen sie eine zum Nachdenken anregende Werkgruppe dar, deren Erforschung überraschende Ergebnisse zutage fördert. Durch die innere und äussere Zwiesprache mit den Werken erlauben sie den Betrachtern die Reflektion über die intimen Zusammenhänge zwischen Leben und Tod, Gesundheit und Krankheit, Kontrolle und Hilflosigkeit.

Scheitern um zum Erfolg zu gelangen

Paddy Hartley hat ein tiefgehendes Interesse am Körper und spezifisch daran, wie Patienten ihre Körper wahrnehmen, wenn sie an einer Krankheit oder Verletzung leiden. Als unternehmerischer Künstler verfügt Paddy über Widerstandskraft und einen kritischen Verstand, was auch bei Roche sehr geschätzt wird. Sein Werk entstammt den Fragen, die er stellt, genau wie die pharmazeutischen Produkte des Unternehmens den Fragen entstammen, die dort gestellt werden. Als Keramiker experimentiert Paddy kontinuierlich und weiss, dass diese Versuche teilweise scheitern werden. In der Tat ist er darauf angewiesen, dass einige dieser Experimente misslingen, um erfolgreiche Werke zu schaffen. Als pharmazeutisches Unternehmen befindet sich Roche in exakt derselben Lage.

PADDY HARTLEY ARBEITET mit komplexen Glasuren, die oftmals faszinierende abstrakte Oberflächenstrukturen erzeugen. Die Abbildung zeigt den Ausschnitt eines Gefässes, das von einer Lavaglasur bedeckt ist.

PADDY HARTLEY WORKS with complex glazes which often create fascinating abstract surface structures. Our image shows a part of a vessel that has been covered with a lava glaze.

Die Werke fordern die Betrachter dazu auf, die intimen Zusammenhänge zwischen Leben und Tod, Gesundheit und Krankheit, Kontrolle und Hilflosigkeit zu reflektieren

A quarter-century of conversations and reflections

Paddy has chosen to make predominant use of white- and red-glazed porcelain paper clay for 'The Cost of Life' collection, making additional use of metal, glass and fabric where appropriate. The artworks vary in scale but are all to be plinth-based. Their inspiration is drawn from the conversations Paddy has conducted over the course of 25 years with patients and medical professionals who have intimate experience of the three chosen themes.

These profound insights are augmented by Paddy's own personal experiences. The artworks articulate his reflections on those conversations, and they also reference one another, so that the themes articulated in one work may appear in some other form in one or more of the other works. A suite of thought-provoking explorations with surprising outcomes, they imply a series of internal and external conversations and encourage the viewer to reflect on the intimate interrelations between life and death, health and illness, control and helplessness.

Failing in order to succeed

Paddy Hartley is deeply interested in the body, and specifically how patients experience their bodies when they suffer illness or injury. As an entrepreneurial artist, Paddy has the resilience and the questioning mind that are valued at Roche. His work derives from the questions he asks, just as the company's pharmaceutical products derive from the questions it asks. As a ceramicist, Paddy experiments all the time and knows that some of these experiments will fail. Indeed, he needs some of those experiments to fail in order to create works that will succeed. As a pharmaceutical company, Roche is in exactly the same position.

DIE ARBEIT MIT TON ist sowohl archaisch als auch technisch herausfordernd. Als uralte Kulturtechnik hat sich die Töpferei kontinuierlich angepasst und macht sich in jeder Epoche neueste Errungenschaften zunutze.

WORKING WITH CLAY is both archaic and technically demanding. As an ancient cultural technique, pottery has continously adapted and utilises the latest advancements of each epoch.

The works of Paddy Hartley encourage the viewer to reflect on the intimate interrelations between life and death, health and illness, control and helplessness

Basel →

Berwick

BAY TERRACE

RG LUXURY MEAT CO

Life is to be treasured. Living, even more so.

Paddy Hartleys Kunst untersucht Themen, wie die Erinnerungskultur, die Ethik in der biomedizinischen Forschung und die Erfahrung, welche Patienten mit Eingriffen an ihren Körpern machen. Er arbeitet mit vielen verschiedenen Medien und Materialien, diese beinhalten auch die Manipulation von Zellgewebe, digitale Fotografie, digitale Stickerei, aber auch die Herstellung von Installationen, Bekleidung und Keramik. Im Folgenden bespricht Paddy seine einzigartige Antwort auf «The Cost of Life» mittels einer Werkgruppe von Keramikkunstwerken.

Paddy Hartley bespricht «The Cost of Life»

Paddy, wie kam es zu dem Projekt «The Cost of Life»?

Einer der bereicherndsten Aspekte meiner Arbeit war die Möglichkeit, während der vergangenen 25 Jahre an Universitäten in Grossbritannien Gastvorlesungen über meine Kunst zu halten. So konnte ich viel von dem, was ich gelernt und erfahren habe, mit der kommenden Generation von Künstlern und Designern teilen. Ein zentraler Rat, den ich geben konnte, ist nicht darauf zu warten, «entdeckt» zu werden. Teilt euch den Leuten mit, sagt, dass ihr und euer Werk existiert und wie ihr und eure Kunst einen Unterschied machen könnt. Es war diese Strategie «mich selbst vorzustellen», die meine Beziehung zum Historischen Archiv Roche, und besonders zu Kurator Alexander Bieri, ermöglichte.

Während mehrerer Gespräche mit Alex stellten wir fest, dass unsere Interessen zu den Bezügen zwischen Wissenschaft, Kunst und dem historischen Kontext nahe beieinander liegen. Ich nahm Alex' Einladung, das Archiv zu besuchen, auf und traf ihn und seine Kolleginnen und Kollegen. Während dieses Besuchs legte mir Alex nahe, den Vorschlag für eine neue Werkgruppe zum 125. Jubiläum von Roche zu erarbeiten. Über die vielen Jahre der Kooperation im Bereich der biomedizinischen Wissenschaften die ich erlebt habe, sowie in zahlreichen Unterhaltungen mit biomedizinischen Forschern, Historikern, Kuratoren, Pflegekräften, Patienten und ihren Familien, strukturierte sich mein Werk stets über eine Geschichte, ein Narrativ, oftmals in Bezug auf eine spezifische Innovation, ein Ereignis oder eine Person. Manchmal ist dieses Narrativ explizit dargestellt, oftmals jedoch in subtilerer Weise.

Zunächst war der natürliche Interessensfokus für mich, die Geschichten hinter einigen der Innovationen in der Pharmazie und Diagnostik, welche die Firma entwickelt hatte, einzubeziehen. Aber Alex riet mir, einen «globaleren» Blickwinkel einzunehmen und unser Vorschlag entwickelte sich in die Richtung, den Einfluss der biomedizinischen Wissenschaften auf die Gesellschaft zu untersuchen. Eine zentrale Quelle der Inspiration dafür war das überaus einflussreiche Symposium zum Thema «The Challenge of Life: Biomedical Progress and Human Values», das aus Anlass des 75. Jubiläums von Roche 1971 durchgeführt worden ist.

Dies löste einen Denkprozess bei mir zum Thema «der Preis des Seins und der Preis des Lebens» (the cost of living and the cost of life) aus. Ich dachte nicht spezifisch an die monetären Kosten des Lebens (auch wenn dies ein gewichtiger Faktor ist), aber viel breiter an unsere Beziehungen mit unserer eigenen Gesundheit und dem Gesundheitssystem, an den Zugang zum Gesundheitswesen, an öffentliche Wahrnehmungen der wissenschaftlichen Forschung und an persönliche Erfahrungen durch Behandlungen und Therapien. Angesichts der Verletzungen (insults) am Körper, wie auch immer sie entstehen mögen, und unter Berücksichtigung der medizinischen Interventionen fragte ich mich — an Stelle der Patienten, aber auch an Stelle der Forscher, der Mediziner und aller anderen, die zu der Erfahrung der Patienten beitragen — was ist der echte «Preis des Seins»?

Life is to be treasured. Living, even more so.

Paddy Hartley's artistic practice investigates themes including memorialisation and remembrance, the ethics of biomedical research, and the patient's experience of insults to the body. He works in a wide range of media including biotissue manipulation and assembly, digital photography, digital embroidery, installation, garment assemblage, and ceramics. Paddy reflects his unique response to 'The Cost of Life' through a unique suite of ceramic artworks.

Paddy Hartley examines 'The Cost of Life'

Paddy, how did the 'Cost of Life' project come about?

One of the most rewarding aspects of the work I do has been the opportunity to guest-lecture about my artistic practice at universities around the UK over the past 25 years or so, sharing much of what I've learned and experienced with the next generation of artists and designers. A key piece of advice I've shared is to not wait to be 'discovered'. Let people know that you and your work exist and how you and your practice can make a difference. It was by employing this strategy of 'introducing myself' that my relationship with the Roche Historical Archive Collection, and specifically with the Curator Alexander Bieri, came about.

Over the course of a series of exchanges with Alex, we realised that our interests in the interrelation of science, art and historical context were very closely aligned. I took up Alex's invitation to visit the Archive and meet him and his colleagues. It was during this visit that Alex suggested I create a proposal for a new body of work to mark Roche's 125th anniversary. Over the many years of biomedical science collaborations I've been involved in, and the many conversations I've had with biomedical innovators, historians, curators, caregivers, patients and their families, my work has always had a storytelling or narrative structure, often relating to the history of a specific innovation, occurrence, person or event. Sometimes this narrative is explicit, but often it is more subtle.

So initially, the natural focus of interest for me was looking at the stories behind some of the innovations in pharmaceuticals and diagnostics developed by the company, and at the people behind those developments. But what Alex was suggesting was to work on something with a more 'global' scope, and our proposal evolved into one examining the impact of biomedical science on society. A key source of initial inspiration for this was the highly influential symposium on the theme 'The Challenge of Life: Biomedical Progress and Human Values' that had been held to mark Roche's 75th Anniversary in 1971.

This set me thinking about 'The Cost of Living and the Cost of Life'. I wasn't thinking specifically about the financial cost of life (although this is a factor), but more broadly about our relationships with our own health and healthcare systems, about access to healthcare, public perceptions of scientific research, and personal experiences of receiving treatments and therapies. In the face of insults to the body, however caused, and taking into account the medical interventions that address them, what is the real 'Cost of Life', I wondered — for the patient, but also for the research scientist, the medical practitioner, and everyone else involved in the patient's experience?

How, then, did you decide to approach this theme?

Exploring the impact of biomedical innovations on society is such a huge subject that the possible ways of addressing it were infinite. I decided to focus on three aspects: the beginning of life, the end of life, and the challenge of

Wie hast Du folglich das Thema angepackt?

Den Einfluss der biomedizinischen Innovationen auf die Gesellschaft zu untersuchen ist so ein enormes Thema, dass die Möglichkeiten, dies zu tun, unendlich sind. Ich beschloss, mich auf drei Aspekte zu beschränken: Den Beginn des Lebens, das Ende des Lebens und die Herausforderung, das Leben qualitativ zu verbessern anstatt es bloss zu verlängern (adding life to years rather than years to life), was für die Philosophie von Roche als Pharmaunternehmen zentral ist.

Der Beginn und das Ende unserer Leben sind die Momente, über die wir am wenigsten Kontrolle haben. Es ist sehr schwierig, Themen zu finden, die für Jeden relevant sind, aber diese beiden Ereignisse sind unausweichliche Elemente jedermanns Leben. Sie wurden zu den Eckpunkten meiner Untersuchung als ich begann, darüber nachzudenken, wie viel Kontrolle wir über unsere Leben während der Dauer unserer Existenz haben — wenn man beispielsweise bedenkt, welche Entscheidungen wir treffen, wie wir Leben in die Welt bringen und auch den Grad der Selbstbestimmtheit darüber, wie unsere Leben enden.

Du warst immer daran interessiert, den Körper über die Kunst zu erkunden. Woher kommt dieses Interesse?

Ich denke, es stammt aus der natürlichen Faszination, die wahrscheinlich die meisten von uns darüber empfinden, wie der Körper funktioniert. Aber ich war zudem stets an der Darstellungsweise des Körperinnern interessiert. Über die Jahre hinweg wuchs mein Interesse daran, wie die Menschen den Körper, den sie bewohnen, ändern — und sich selbst als menschliche Wesen auch als Antwort auf diese Erfahrungen verändern, sei es durch Design, Krankheit, Unfall oder Gewalt. Diese Faszination packte mich richtig, als ich damit begann, die Geschichte der rekonstruktiven Gesichtschirurgie zu erforschen, spezifisch die Arbeit von Harold Gillies in Sidcup, der Kriegsveteranen des Ersten Weltkriegs behandelte. Die Patienten von Gillies hatten alle eine gemeinsame Erfahrung, nicht nur des Kriegs, sondern auch der rekonstruktiven Chirurgie, die in jenen Tagen der Entstehung dieses Gebiets notgedrungen zu einem gewissen Grad experimentell war. Für viele von ihnen war es nicht klar, ob die chirurgischen Eingriffe zu einem funktionierenden Gesicht führen und noch viel weniger, ob das rekonstruierte Gesicht demjenigen von vor der Verletzung ähnlich sehen würde. Somit stellte sich auch die Frage, ob sie sich wieder in die Gesellschaft eingliedern und ein Anstellungsverhältnis finden können, um ihre Familien zu versorgen.

Mein erstes Interesse galt der Chirurgie selbst — und ich bin immer noch verblüfft, wie erfolgreich sie war — aber nach einer gewissen Zeit verschob es sich zu der Erfahrung der Patienten, die ihr unterzogen worden waren. Wie lebten diese Leute weiter, nachdem, was ihnen zustiess? Dies war ein Zeitalter, in dem erworbene Behinderungen viel häufiger vorkamen als heute, weil so viele junge Menschen im Krieg verletzt worden waren. Aber die grosse Mehrheit dieser Männer waren keine Berufssoldaten; sie waren ganz normale Menschen — Bäcker, Schuhmacher, Händler — und sie kamen alle aus sehr unterschiedlichen Verhältnissen.

Über meine Nachforschungen und das Auffinden von Familienmitgliedern einer ausgewählten Gruppe von etwa 5000 Soldaten fand ich heraus, dass viele von ihnen sehr unauffällige, bescheidene Leben führten; nach dem Horror der Schützengräben war dies alles, was sie sich wünschten. Ich war fasziniert von den Herausforderungen denen sie sich in ihrem Versuch, eine normale Existenz wiederaufzunehmen, gegenübersahen. Viele Familienmitglieder sprechen davon, wie fürsorglich sie sich um ihre Väter, Onkel und Grossväter gekümmert hatten, die nach der plastischen Chirurgie als unterschiedliche physische und psychologische Version ihrer selbst hervorgingen. Sie wurden älter und wuchsen sozusagen in ihre neu zusammengesetzten Gesichter hinein, womit ihre chirurgisch veränderten Gesichter länger zu ihnen gehörten, als diejenigen von vor der Verletzung. Je älter sie wurden, desto weniger stark waren die Verletzungen sichtbar. Und viele dieser Männer begannen immer mehr, ihre veränderte Erscheinung zu akzeptieren, da sie sich mit ihr angefreundet hatten. Was ihnen wirklich wichtig war, war die Akzeptanz ihrer Familien und des Umfelds. Diese persönlichen Geschichten veränderten grundlegend den Fokus der Untersuchung meines Themas als Künstler. Es waren nicht unsere Körper per se, die mich interessierten, sondern die Erfahrung der Menschen, die diese bewohnten.

Als ich diesen Auftrag begann, war mein ursprünglicher Ansatz, mit vielen Leuten zu sprechen, die mit diversen medizinischen Leiden und

adding life to years rather than years to life, which is fundamental to the philosophy of Roche as a pharmaceutical company.

The beginning and the end of our lives are the moments over which we have the least control. It's very difficult to find subjects that are relevant to everybody, but those two subjects are unavoidable elements in everyone's lives. They became the cornerstones of my investigation as I started to reflect on how much control we have over our lives during the span of our existence — thinking, for instance, of the choices we make about how we bring life into the world and also of the degree of choice that we have, or do not have, about how our lives end.

You've always been interested in exploring the body through art. Where does this interest spring from?

I suppose it came from that natural fascination I think most of us have with how the body works, but I was always additionally interested in how the internal body is depicted. Over the years, I became increasingly interested in the way people can change the bodies they occupy, and can themselves change as human beings in response to these experiences, whether by design, illness, accident or through violence. This fascination really took hold once I began researching the history of facial reconstructive surgery, specifically the work carried out by Harold Gillies in Sidcup on servicemen injured during the First World War. Gillies' patients all had a common experience, not just of war but of going through reconstructive procedures which, certainly in the early days, involved a degree of calculated experimentation born of necessity. For many of them, it was not clear whether the surgery they were undergoing would result in a fully functioning face, let alone whether the reconstructed face would resemble their pre-injury face, or whether they would be able to fit back into society after recovery and gain employment to support their families.

My initial interest was in the surgery itself — and I'm still staggered by how successful it was — but in the course of time, it shifted to the experience of the patients who had undergone it. How did these people go on living after what had happened to them? This was an age in which acquired disability was far more common than it is today, because so many people had been injured in the War, but the vast majority of these men weren't professional soldiers: they were just ordinary people — bakers, shoemakers, tradesmen, and all from very differing backgrounds.

Through my research and tracing of family members of a select group numbering more than 5000 servicemen, I discovered that many of them went on to live very quiet, humble lives; that was really all they wanted after the horrors of the trenches. I was fascinated by the challenges they underwent in trying to resume a normal existence. Many family members speak of how protective they were of their fathers, uncles and grandfathers, who emerged from the plastic surgery unit as a different version of themselves, physically and psychologically. As they grew older and 'into' their faces, this post-surgery face had been theirs longer than their pre-injury face and grew into their reassembled faces as they got older. The more they aged, the less evident the injuries became. And many of these men became increasingly accepting of their altered appearance through gradual familiarity. Acceptance by their families and communities was what really mattered to them. It was those personal stories that really changed the focus of my examination of my subject. It wasn't our bodies as such that interested me, but the experience of the people who inhabited them.

So my original approach when embarking on this commission had been to speak with a wide range of people who had experience of various medical conditions and therapeutic interventions and to draw on their experiences and insights. But establishing these relationships and building trust with contributors from whom you are hoping to glean often very personal experiences takes time and calls for face-to-face interactions. Researching this and making the process work during a global pandemic has its challenges, and although Zoom meetings have been a lifeline for many families and friends, it wasn't conducive to my usual approach to trust-building with contributors. Usually I would spend years building these relationships and creating the artistic responses, but given the COVID-19 pandemic and the limited time available to research and create the work, I quickly realised that I would have to shift my approach. It began to dawn on me that in the course of all my work during 25 years of artistic practice, I've always focused on the stories of others rather than my own experiences. This has been a deliberate choice: I believe that a lot of contemporary art is excessively self-referential and inward-looking, and

therapeutischen Interventionen Erfahrung hatten und ihre Einsichten einzubeziehen. Aber es braucht Zeit und persönliche Interaktion, um diese Beziehungen aufzubauen und das Vertrauen der Mitwirkenden zu gewinnen, von denen man oftmals sehr persönliche Erfahrungen zu vernehmen hofft. Diesen Ansatz während einer Pandemie zu verfolgen ist eine Herausforderung und auch wenn Zoom-Konferenzen für viele Familien und Freunde zu einem rettenden Anker wurden, war dies meinem üblichen Vorgehen, um Vertrauen aufzubauen, abträglich. Üblicherweise hätte ich Jahre damit verbracht, diese Beziehungen und die künstlerischen Antworten darauf zu entwickeln. Aber mit der COVID-19 Pandemie und der begrenzten zur Verfügung stehenden Zeit, um das Werk zu recherchieren und zu schaffen, realisierte ich rasch, dass ich mein Vorgehen anpassen muss.

Langsam dämmerte mir, dass ich mich im Laufe meiner 25 Jahre währenden künstlerischen Tätigkeit immer auf die Geschichten anderer fokussiert hatte, statt auf meine eigenen Erfahrungen. Dies war eine bewusste Entscheidung: Ich glaube, ein Grossteil der zeitgenössischen Kunst ist exzessiv selbst-referentiell und introspektiv angelegt und ich scheute mich jahrelang davor, diesen Ansatz zu verfolgen. Aber aufbauend auf den Erkenntnissen, die ich aus der Arbeit mit Menschen im Gesundheitswesen gewonnen hatte — genauso wie meine eigenen Erfahrungen, die lebensbedrohliche Erkrankungen und den Entzug von Gesundheitsfürsorge gegen meinen eigenen Willen beinhalten — realisierte ich, dass es Zeit war, nebst anderen meine eigene Stimme in mein Werk einfliessen zu lassen.

Du hast über den Lauf Deiner Karriere mit vielen verschiedenen Materialien und Techniken gearbeitet. Wieso und warum hast Du Dich für das spezifische Material für «The Cost of Life» entschieden?

Ich habe viele verschiedene Materialien und Techniken über die Jahre erforscht und ausprobiert und stets die geeignetsten Materialien, Prozesse und Techniken für die Schaffung meiner Werke angewandt. Doch meine Ausbildung genoss ich als Keramiker und es ist das erste Material, in das ich mich wirklich verliebt habe. Über die vergangenen fünf Jahre bin ich praktisch ausschliesslich zur Arbeit mit Ton zurückgekehrt — wiederum, weil dieser so unglaublich vielgestaltig ist. Seltsamer- und unerwarteterweise war es die Arbeit mit Lammherz-Gewebe für meine Installation «Papaver Rhoeas» am King's College, die meine Begeisterung für Ton wieder aufflammen liess. Fleisch, Muskel und Gewebe haben eine annähernd plastische Qualität wenn man mit ihnen arbeitet. Selbst wenn Gewebe faktisch tot ist, fühlte es sich für mich aufgrund seiner organischen Natur recht gegensätzlich an. Viele Leute, die mit Ton arbeiten, werden Dir erzählen, dass es einen bestimmten «sweet spot» gibt, bei dem das Material lebendig wird und ich hatte dieselbe Empfindung, als ich mit den Lammherzen umging.

Sowohl während meiner Studien- als auch meiner Hochschulzeit als Keramiker am Institut der University of Wales in Cardiff, wurden wir aktiv dazu aufgefordert, nebst unserem primären Werkstoff andere Materialien einzubeziehen. So experimentierte ich mit einer Unzahl verschiedener Medien, aber als ich begann, mit Ton zu arbeiten, realisierte ich, wie ausserordentlich vielfältig dieser ist. Wenn man sich die Zeit nimmt, kann man alles damit anstellen und ihn wie alles Mögliche aussehen lassen. Er kann unglaublich herausfordernd sein, gleichzeitig verzeiht er vieles. Doch gibt es so viel, was man mit Ton anstellen kann, dass die Möglichkeiten grenzenlos sind. Besonders, wenn man ihn mit Glasuren kombiniert, die mittels Brenntemperatur, Brennatmosphäre, Brennstoffen und vor allem Technik adaptiert werden, ist die Vielfalt unendlich. Wenn ich ganz ehrlich bin, habe ich nicht immer Vergnügen an der Arbeit mit all den Materialien und Prozessen empfunden, aber sie waren notwendig für das jeweilige Werk, an dem ich gerade sass. Bei diesem Auftrag wollte ich wirklich mit einem Material arbeiten, das mir Spass macht. Ich wollte zurück dazu, mit Ton zu arbeiten und ihn wieder lieben zu lernen — und die Entscheidung ist die Beste, die ich seit langer Zeit getroffen habe.

Die Mehrzahl der Werke, die ich für diesen Auftrag herstelle, sind in Porzellanpapier ausgeführt, das im ungebrannten Zustand ein sehr dankbares Material ist, aber im Brennprozess grosse Schwierigkeiten mit sich bringt. Alle Porzellane haben eine enorme Schwundrate, sie verlieren nahezu 20 Prozent des Umfangs verglichen vom nassen Rohzustand zum Hochtemperaturbrand bei 1300 Grad Celsius. Es verformt und bewegt sich, wenn es einen nahezu glasartigen

I've shied away from this approach for many years. But based on the experiences I've had working with people in healthcare scenarios — as well as my own experiences, which include life-threatening health issues and what it means to be opted out of healthcare against my will — it occurred to me that it was time to start putting my own voice into my work alongside the voices of others.

You have worked across a wide range of materials and techniques over the course of your career. How and why have you chosen the specific media you are using for 'The Cost of Life'?

I've explored and utilised a wide range of materials and techniques over the years, and I've always applied the most appropriate material, process and technique to the creation of my work. Yet my training is in ceramics, and it's the first material I truly fell in love with. During the past five years or so, I've returned to working almost exclusively in clay once again because it's so incredibly versatile. Curiously, and rather unexpectedly, it was working with lamb's-heart tissue for my 'Papaver Rhoeas' project at King's College London that renewed my passion for clay. Flesh, muscle and tissue have an almost plastic quality when you work with them. Even though the tissue is to all intents and purposes dead, to me it felt quite the opposite in its organic nature. Many people who work in clay will tell you that there's a certain 'sweet spot' in it where the material becomes alive, and I started to experience this when working with the lambs' hearts.

During both my undergraduate and post-graduate studies in Ceramics at University of Wales Institute, Cardiff, we were actively encouraged to explore and incorporate other materials alongside our primary media, I'd experimented with so many different media, but when I started working with clay, I realised how extraordinarily versatile it is. Given time, you can do anything with it and make it look like anything. It can be incredibly challenging and at the same time forgiving, but there's so much you can do with clay, and the possibilities are infinite: particularly when you start to combine it with glazes, firing temperatures, firing atmospheres, combustibles and above all technique, the variety is endless. If I'm absolutely frank, I haven't always enjoyed all the materials and processes I've worked with in the past, but they've always been necessary for the work I've been making. I really wanted to enjoy the material I would be using for this commission. I wanted to get back into working with and loving clay again — and that decision is the best one I've made for a long time.

The majority of the work I'm making for this commission uses porcelain paper clay, which can be a very forgiving material to work with in its unfired state but is incredibly challenging to fire. Any porcelain has a huge shrinkage rate, up to 20 percent from its raw plastic condition to its high-fired state at 1300 degrees Celsius. It warps and moves as it nears its glass-like state, and it becomes even more challenging when you start to combine glaze with it. I'm taking huge risks working with porcelain because it can be so very unpredictable. That said, I've deliberately set certain pieces up to fail because in some instances, it's right for the aesthetic of those specific pieces. But more crucially, I need to see exactly how something will fail in order to achieve an understanding of how to succeed with subsequent pieces. And I don't regard the notion of failure as a negative. On the contrary, those set-ups for failure are based on my knowledge that the clay will behave a particular way in the firing, and I can exploit that to my advantage.

Each group of works I'm creating uses a different building method, different techniques and ways of manipulating and assembling the work, be it throwing on the wheel, slip-casting liquid clay, assembling from clay extrusions, modelling, or slab-building. Most of the work will be glazed white or red, but in a wide variety of surface qualities, and each will subsequently require a different firing schedule. All of this involves an extraordinary amount of testing to ensure I get exactly the results I'm aiming for.

What does your studio mean to you, Paddy and the working environment you create for your-self?

Here, in my home studio in Berwick-upon-Tweed? I feel completely free to experiment and to try out new techniques. To work with clay and glaze with no restrictions. In the studio I've created here, I've rediscovered that

Zustand annimmt und das Ganze wird noch anspruchsvoller, wenn man beginnt, die Stücke zu glasieren.

Ich gehe mit Porzellan grosse Risiken ein, da das Material so unvorhersehbar sein kann. Davon abgesehen habe ich aus Absicht viele Stücke so gemacht, dass sie misslingen werden, weil dies in manchen Fällen der Ästhetik dieser spezifischen Werke gut tut. Aber noch wesentlicher ist, dass ich genau erkennen muss, wie etwas schief geht, um zu verstehen, wie ich mit den nachfolgenden Stücken Erfolge erzielen kann. Und ich sehe die Idee des Scheiterns nicht als negativ an: Ganz im Gegenteil, dieses konzipierte Scheitern beruht auf meinem Wissen, dass sich der Ton während des Brandes in einer bestimmten Weise verhält und so kann ich diese Erfahrungen zu meinem Vorteil nutzen.

Jede Werkgruppe, die ich schaffe, benötigt eine unterschiedliche Aufbautechnik, unterschiedliche Techniken und Wege, die Werke zu handhaben und zusammenzusetzen. Sei es das Zentrieren und Drehen auf der Töpferscheibe, das Giessen von geschlämmtem Ton, das Zusammensetzen stranggepresster Tonstücke, das Modellieren oder der Aufbau mittels Tonplatten. Die meisten Werke werden weiss oder rot glasiert, sind aber in vielen verschiedenen Oberflächenqualitäten ausgeführt, wodurch jedes ein unterschiedliches Brennprogramm erfordert. All dies benötigt eine aussergewöhnliche Menge an Tests, um sicherzustellen, dass ich genau die gewünschten Resultate erhalte.

Was bedeutet Dir Dein Studio, Paddy, und das Arbeitsumfeld, das Du für Dich selbst schaffst?

Hier, in meinem Heimstudio in Berwick-upon-Tweed? Ich fühle mich hier komplett frei, zu experimentieren und neue Techniken auszuprobieren. Mit Ton und Glasuren ohne Restriktionen zu arbeiten. Im Studio, welches ich hier aufgebaut habe, entdeckte ich die Begeisterung wieder, die ich erstmals vor über 30 Jahren verspürte, als ich mein Studium als Keramiker begann. Und ich spüre, dass es noch viel mehr zu entdecken gibt. Es dreht sich darum, eine neue und doch vertraute kreative Seele entdeckt zu haben. Als ich Gastvorlesungen durchführte, habe ich oft von etwas gesprochen, das ich als «schöpferische Angst» bezeichnet habe. Dies ist eine ganz normale Sache, die alle kreativen Menschen empfinden, aber niemand spricht darüber oder akzeptiert es. Der Ausdruck der Erleichterung auf den Gesichtern meiner Zuhörer, wenn ich ihnen aufzeige, wie ich selbst mit meiner schöpferischen Angst umgehe, ist eine der bereicherndsten Erfahrungen dieser Gastvorlesungen — die Erkenntnis, dass es OK ist, wenn man sich vor Beginn einer neuen Arbeit ängstigt oder nervös ist.

Für mich persönlich gilt, dass ich meine Arbeit und diese sogenannten Misserfolge unter Ausschluss der Öffentlichkeit machen möchte. Doch sind es eben keine Misserfolge, denn so lerne ich dazu und kann die Werke entwickeln. Und um mir hier selbst zu widersprechen, am Ende zeige ich sie dann doch den Leuten, denn dabei handelt es ich um einen Teil des Entwicklungs- und Evolutionsprozesses eines Stückes. Dieser kundig geplante «scheitern-um-zum-Erfolg-zu-gelangen» Ansatz spiegelt sich natürlich in der Erforschung und Entwicklung von Pharmazeutika wieder. Jedes Atelier, das ich je hatte, war für andere Menschen zugänglich, sei es beispielsweise ein Zahnlabor oder ein Gemeinschaftsatelier oder der Teil einer alten Bibliothek. Immer waren andere Leute da. Aber ich fühle mich so viel behaglicher, alleine zu arbeiten. Du kannst Dir nicht vorstellen, wie sehr ich die Ausgangssperre genossen habe.

Es ist so: Wenn ich mit einer Arbeit zum ersten Mal beginne, bin ich ungemein unzufrieden mit meinen frühen Herangehensweisen an das Stück, und ich muss dies wohl oder übel als Teil des Prozesses akzeptieren. Aber es ist notwendig, diesen Weg zu beschreiten. Ich muss dies tun, um herauszufinden, was ich denn nun eigentlich in welcher Art herstellen werde. Dies in den eigenen vier Wänden tun zu können, ist sehr befreiend, denn so muss ich nicht um die Meinung anderer zu einem Stück in frühem Entwicklungszustand besorgt sein.

Und alleine in meinem eigenen privaten Umfeld zu arbeiten, hat auch mit sich gebracht, dass ich in den letzten sechs Monaten Techniken ausprobieren konnte, an die ich mich vorher nie gewagt habe. Meiner Meinung nach sollte ein guter Künstler immer ein Lernender sein. Manche meiner Experimente gingen gut und andere nicht, aber es hat mir auch das Selbstvertrauen gegeben, Dinge zu vereinfachen. Der aktuelle Trend in der zeitgenössischen Keramik geht in Richtung Überdekoration,

excitement I first experienced when I began my training in Ceramics over 30 years ago. And I feel that there's so much to discover. It's about having rediscovered a new but familiar creative self. When I used to guest-lecture, I often spoke of something I call 'maker's fear'. It's a perfectly normal thing to experience as a creative, but nobody talks about or acknowledges it. The look of relief on the faces of my audience when I discussed how I deal with my own maker's fear was one of the most rewarding parts of delivering those guest lectures — the realisation that it's OK to be scared or nervous about starting a new body of work from scratch. Personally, I like to make my work and have those so-called failures in private, but really they aren't failures because this is how I learn and how I develop the work. And to contradict myself, I end up showing them to people, because it's all part of the build and evolution of a piece. This informed 'fail-to-succeed' approach is mirrored in pharmaceutical research and development, of course.

Every studio space I've ever had has been accessible to other people, whether it's been a dental laboratory, for instance, or a group studio, or part of an old library. There have always been other people around. But I feel so much more comfortable working in isolation. You can imagine I've very much enjoyed lockdown. The thing is, I know when I start working on something for the first time that I'll be intensely dissatisfied with my early versions of the piece, and I've accepted this as part of the process, but it is essential I take this approach. I need to do this in order to figure out what it is I'm actually going to make and how I'm going to make it. Doing it in a private space is very liberating, because it means I don't have to be concerned about the views others may have of the piece in its early gestation.

And working in isolation, in my own private space, has meant that there are techniques I've tried with clay in the past six months that I've never attempted before. I feel a good artist should always be a student. Some of my experiments have gone well and others haven't, but it's also given me the confidence to simplify things. The current trend in much contemporary work in ceramics is over-embellished, or else incorporates an inordinate amount of detail in the work — what I call a 'detail vomit'. I want to do the precise opposite. Keep it simple. Pare it down. Focus on the message of the work and keep it really clear and above all, unanticipated. Give the viewer something they aren't expecting.

What does it mean to be an artist, in your view?

Speaking from a personal perspective, it's a discipline that allows me to explore and interweave research, practice and often collaboration with people I may never have encountered personally, responding to any subject I choose, and to interpret that subject in a way that I hope hasn't been seen before. It allows me to address and pose really challenging questions, and to present experiences that the viewer may not have had — or on the contrary, which they may relate to intensely. And the viewer may well respond to that presentation in ways I might not have anticipated myself. Without exception, the way an audience responds to something I make always surprises me, and occasionally I find it utterly disarming.

Because I know how satisfying it is to come up with an idea for a piece, to develop it, to figure out how to make it, and then to present it to people, I'll always try to get anyone I know to try making things. During lockdown, I'm sending friends a bag of clay and saying, "Here's some clay. Don't worry about firing it: just make something with it!" It's fascinating to see how quickly people realise just how challenging working with clay can be but also how rewarding the tactility and the experience can be.

I think that at times in the past, I've tended to have had so much respect for the subject-matter I've been dealing with, and so much respect for the people I've been working with, that I've actually stopped having fun with the making process, and fun is actually a huge part of what I do. That's why I always like to try to incorporate a little bit humour in my work, no matter how serious the subject — but only where it is appropriate, so as to not be misinterpreted. It's not that I don't take it seriously — I take my work and the subjects I address very seriously — but that element of fun and enjoyment is so important, because without it, I don't think you're going to make good work. The more you enjoy the process, the better your work will be, in my opinion. And people will immediately recognise that enjoyment in your work. When I do really get down to work on a piece, I work very fast. The more I think about a piece of work, the more contrived it feels.

oder auch der übermässigen Detaillierung der Stücke — was ich «Detail-Erbrechen» nenne. Ich möchte genau das Gegenteil davon tun. Halte es einfach. Reduziere es. Fokussiere Dich auf die Botschaft des Werks und halte diese wirklich klar und vor allem unvorhersehbar. Gib den Betrachtern etwas, das sie nicht erwarten.

Was bedeutet es Deiner Ansicht nach, ein Künstler zu sein?

Aus meiner persönlichen Perspektive ist es eine Disziplin, die mir erlaubt, Forschung, Handwerk und oftmals die Zusammenarbeit mit Menschen, die ich sonst nie persönlich kennengelernt hätte, zu ergründen und zu verknüpfen; auf ein Thema, das ich ausgesucht habe, zu antworten und dieses in einer Art zu interpretieren, von der ich hoffe, dass sie nie zuvor so gesehen worden sei. Es erlaubt mir, wirklich herausfordernde Fragen zu stellen und Erfahrungen anzubieten, die für die Betrachter neu sind — oder im Gegenteil, zu denen sie eine starke Beziehung haben. Und der Betrachter mag oftmals in einer Art auf meine Werke reagieren, die ich selbst nicht vorhergesehen habe. Die Art, wie ein Publikum auf etwas reagiert, was ich gemacht habe, überrascht mich stets und ohne Ausnahme, manchmal finde ich die Reaktionen überraschend schlüssig.

Da ich weiss, wie befriedigend es ist, eine Idee für ein Stück zu entwickeln, herauszufinden, wie man es herstellt und es dann Menschen zu zeigen, versuche ich stets, meine Bekannten dazu zu bewegen, Dinge herstellen zu versuchen. Während der Ausgangssperre sandte ich Freunden Säcke mit Ton und sagte ihnen: «Hier hast Du Ton. Sorge Dich nicht darum, wie man die Sachen brennt, mache einfach etwas damit!» Es ist faszinierend, dass die Leute sehr rasch merken, wie schwierig die Arbeit mit Ton ist, aber auch, wie befriedigend der taktile Umgang damit und die Erfahrung an sich sein kann.

Ich denke, in der Vergangenheit habe ich manchmal vor meinem Sachgebiet und den Menschen, mit denen ich gearbeitet habe, zu viel Respekt gehabt — so sehr, dass mir die Freude am Gestalten abhanden gekommen ist, und Freude daran ist tatsächlich ein riesiger Teil dessen, was ich tue. Das ist der Grund, weswegen ich immer gerne etwas Humor in mein Werk einfliessen lasse, unabhängig davon, wie ernst das Thema scheint — aber nur wo es angebracht ist, damit man mich nicht missversteht. Es geht nicht darum, dass ich es nicht ernst nehmen würde — ich nehme mein Werk und die Themen, die ich behandle sehr ernst — aber Freude und Vergnügen sind wichtig, weil man sonst keine gute Arbeit machen kann. Je mehr man den Prozess an sich geniesst, desto besser wird meiner Meinung nach das Werk herauskommen. Und die Menschen werden die Freude in deinem Werk sofort erkennen. Wenn ich mich dann an die Arbeit mache, geht es sehr schnell. Je mehr ich über ein Stück nachdenke, desto gekünstelter wirkt es.

Was bedeutet es Dir, als Künstler erfolgreich zu sein?

Es gibt so viele verschiedene Aspekte des Erfolgs. Es hört sich wohl etwas abgeschmackt an, aber Freude an der Arbeit zu haben, bedeutet für mich Erfolg — wirklich Freude daran zu haben und auch die Erleichterung, wenn man die endgültige Form präsentieren kann. Die Erleichterung, ein Stück zu beenden, ist vermutlich die grösste Befriedigung — besonders, wenn man mit Keramik arbeitet, weil da so viele Dinge im Auge behalten werden müssen, damit ein Werk gelingt. Es geht auch um den Aspekt des Erfolgsgefühls, die Elemente Inspiration, Materialien und Techniken in einer Weise kombiniert zu haben, die ein Publikum in ihren Bann zieht, und Themen sowie Geschichten beinhaltet, welche es noch nie gesehen und so nicht erwartet hätte. Und natürlich bedeutet Erfolg für mich auch, Werke zu schaffen, die den Menschen Freude bereiten und die sie gerne bei sich zu Hause haben möchten.

Und was bedeutet es, zu scheitern?

Ich schaue auf einige der Werke, die ich über die Jahre gemacht habe zurück und sehe heute, dass ich sie anders hätte herstellen können. Ich denke, da gibt es einige Aspekte, die ich revidieren könnte — und in der Tat nehme ich in einigen Fällen Änderungen vor. Wenn es etwas gibt, was ich gemacht habe und es stimmt nicht ganz, bin ich absolut glücklich damit, darauf zurückzugreifen — sei es auch 20 Jahre später. Es mag sein, dass ich mich heute kompetenter darin fühle, ein bestimmtes Problem zu lösen und dass ich ein besseres Verständnis des Themas, des Materials oder der Technik habe, sowie was dazu benötigt wird, das Stück zu

So what does it mean to you to succeed as an artist?

There are so many different aspects of success. It may sound predictable, but enjoying what I make means success for me — really enjoying it, and also the relief of presenting it in its final form. The relief of finishing a piece is probably the most rewarding part — especially when you're working with ceramics, for there are so many things you have to get right for a piece to work. There's also the aspect of feeling like I've succeeded in combining inspirations, materials and techniques to produce something that engages an audience, presenting subjects and stories they may not have encountered and in ways they hadn't anticipated. And of course success for me also means making work that people enjoy, and that they appreciate having in their homes.

And what does it mean to fail?

I look back on some of the things I've made over the years and think now that I could have executed them differently. I think that there are certain aspects that I could revise — and indeed, in some cases, I actually do go back and revise them. If there's something I've made that doesn't sit quite right, I'm more than happy to revisit it — even as much as 20 years later. It may be that I feel more capable now that I was then of solving a particular problem, and that I have a better understanding of the subject, the material or technique and what is necessary to resolve the piece. In Ceramics, there are always failures. It's part and parcel of the process. But for myself, I need to get things wrong in order to get things right.

What are you learning through this project, Paddy?

I'm learning every day, but there's so much to do and so little time. This project is a response to many things, whether it's age-related disease, attitudes towards euthanasia, the rationale behind the development of the contraceptive pill, or the way in which IVF and gene therapy are developing. It's informed by everything I'm alarmed about, reassured about, outraged about and hopeful of. One consequence of this commission is that I'm beginning to realise that I'm probably not going to have enough time in my life to do all the things I want to do. The experience of the past six months creating this new body of work has required me to think in many new ways about how to conceive the work, how to build it, and how to fire it. It makes me realise that no matter how experienced you might be, there's always so much more to learn and discover. Now I'm thinking, "Hmmn… Some of those quality-of-life-extending treatments that people are wishing for — I could probably do with one or two of them myself!" There's so much I still want to do, and I'm working as fast as I can to learn as much as I can.

A final question. What does 'The Cost of Life' mean to you?

All the work I've been making could be interpreted as being inspired by both living and dying, which are essentially the same thing, if you apply this to a biological form. For me, however, there's a very distinct difference between 'Life' and 'Living'. The 'Cost of Life' is that to sustain life, at all costs, can be to the detriment of 'living'. Living is what life facilitates. Life gives us that 'jumping-off point' from which we can experience living. When we undertake measures, particularly at the end of a life, to extend that life at all costs, often the experience of living and the quality of that living are either degraded or almost entirely ignored. In the worst cases, they're abused. The living experience becomes a form of abuse, disregarding the wishes and the quality of life of the person whose life is being extended beyond its natural end-point, for the sake of preserving that life.

Life is to be treasured. Living, even more so. Dying and the individual dying experience must be respected and, come the time, embraced.

Paddy Hartley was interviewed by Jonathan Steffen in March 2021.

berichtigen. Bei der Keramik gibt es immer Ausschuss. Es ist ein integraler Bestandteil des Prozesses. Aber für mich ist es so, dass ich Fehler machen muss, um die Dinge richtig hinzubekommen.

Was lernst Du durch dieses Projekt, Paddy?

Ich lerne täglich, aber es gibt soviel zu tun und viel zu wenig Zeit. Dieses Projekt ist eine Erwiderung auf viele Dinge, seien es altersbedingte Krankheiten, Haltungen gegenüber der Euthanasie, die Überlegungen hinter der Entwicklung der oralen Kontrazeptiva oder auch die Art, wie sich IVF (In-Vitro-Fertilisation) und Gentherapie entwickeln. Es ist beeinflusst durch alles, was mich beunruhigt, beruhigt, empört und zuversichtlich stimmt.

Eine Folge dieses Auftrags ist, dass ich erkenne, nicht genug Zeit für alles zu haben, was ich in meinem Leben tun möchte. Die Erfahrung, während der letzten sechs Monate diese Werkgruppe zu schaffen, erfoderte von mir, in vielerlei neuen Pfaden über die Konzeption, die Schaffung und das Brennen der Werke nachzudenken. Dadurch verstehe ich nun, dass unabhängig von der Erfahrung, die man haben mag, immer noch viel zu lernen und zu entdecken ist. So denke ich jetzt: «Hmmm... Einige dieser von vielen Menschen erwünschten Behandlungen, die die Qualität des Lebens verbessern — ich könnte womöglich selbst das eine oder andere davon gebrauchen!» Es gibt so viel, was ich noch tun möchte, und ich arbeite so schnell ich nur kann, um so viel wie möglich zu lernen.

Eine letzte Frage. Was bedeutet Dir «The Cost of Life»?

All die Werke, die ich mache, könnten als durch Leben und Tod inspiriert interpretiert werden, was beides grundsätzlich dasselbe darstellt, wenn man es aus biologischer Sicht betrachtet. Allerdings gibt es für mich einen merklichen Unterschied zwischen «Leben als Existenz» (life) und «Leben als Spiel der Möglichkeiten» (living). Der «Preis des Seins» (Cost of Life) ist, dass die Aufrechterhaltung des «Lebens als Existenz» (life) dem «Leben als Spiel der Möglichkeiten» (living) abträglich sein kann. Das «Leben als Spiel der Möglichkeiten» benötigt als Grundlage das «Leben als Existenz». Das «Leben als Existenz» gibt uns den Ausgangspunkt, von dem weg wir das «Leben als Spiel der Möglichkeiten» erfahren können. Wenn wir Massnahmen ergreifen, besonders am Ende des Lebens, um dieses Leben um jeden Preis zu verlängern, stehen die Erfahrungen des «Lebens als Spiel der Möglichkeiten» und die Qualität dieses Lebens oftmals hintan. In den schlimmsten Fällen werden sie gar missbraucht. Die Erfahrung des Lebens als «Spiel der Möglichkeiten» kann durch die Missachtung der Wünsche und der Lebensqualität der Person, deren Leben um des Erhalts desselben willen über den natürlichen Endpunkt hinaus fortgesetzt wird, missbraucht werden.

Das «Leben als Existenz» ist wertvoll. Noch mehr jedoch das «Leben als Spiel der Möglichkeiten». Sterben und die individuelle Erfahrung von sterben sind zu respektieren und — wenn die Zeit da ist — anzunehmen.

Paddy Hartley wurde im März 2021 durch Jonathan Steffen interviewt.

Paddy Hartley

Paddy Hartley: Biographie

«The Cost of Life», von Roche 2020 beauftragt, ist Paddys erste Ausstellung von Keramiken und auch seine erste Retrospektive.

Das Werk von Paddy Hartley wird international ausgestellt, gesammelt und publiziert. Seine künstlerische Arbeit ergründet Themen der Erinnerungskultur wie «Informationen speichern oder Erinnern». Er hat auch den Diskurs zwischen Glaubensgruppen sowie biomedizinische Forschung, die Ethik des humanen Klonens und den Gebrauch und Missbrauch von Steroiden im Kraftsport untersucht. Er arbeitet in den unterschiedlichsten Medien, wie der Manipulation biologischen Gewebes, digitaler Fotografie, digitaler Stickerei, der Herstellung von Installationen, Textilien und Bekleidung, und natürlich auch von Keramik.

Paddy war unter anderem *Visiting Senior Research Fellow* im «Department of Tissue Engineering & Biophotonics» am King's College London und *Artist in Residence* am «National Maritime Museum», London. Etliche von Paddys Arbeiten wurden mit Unterstützung des Wellcome Trust geschaffen. Die daraus hervorgegangenen Projekte beinhalten die Gestaltung und Herstellung seiner die Erscheinung modifizierenden «Gesichtskorsette», die Herstellung von Gesichtsimplantaten aus Bioglas für den klinischen Gebrauch und seine Interpretationen für das Projekt «Façade» — eine Reaktion auf die chirurgischen und persönlichen Geschichten von Veteranen des Ersten Weltkriegs mit Gesichtsverletzungen. Eine Übersicht seines Werks — «Paddy Hartley: Of Faces and Facades» von David Houston Jones und Marjorie Gehrhardt — erschien 2015 im Black Dog Publishing (London) Verlag.

Paddy arbeitete eng mit Wegbereitern aus dem Grenzgebiet der Wissenschaft und der Kunst zusammen, darunter dem Bioglas/Biomaterialien-Forscher Dr. Ian Thompson (King's College London, KCL); dem einstigen Kurator des Gillies Archiv Dr. Andrew Bamji; dem Kurator des Gordon Museum of Anatomy am KCL William Edwards; und Professor Malcolm Logan, der Randall Division of Cell and Molecular Biophysics, ebenfalls am KCL.

Paddy hat auch massgeschneiderte Gesichtskorsette und Halsbekleidung für Privatkunden geschaffen, beispielsweise für Lady Gaga, Noomi Rapace, Elizabeth Banks, Georgia May Jagger, Richard Sawdon Smith, Simon Foxton, Edward Enninful, Jacob K und Jonathan Kaye. Seine Designstücke wurden in führenden Modemagazinen gezeigt, darunter AnOther Magazine, Vogue Italien/China/Deutschland/Türkei, V Magazine, W Magazine, Interview, The Hunger und Harpers China. Seine Arbeiten wurden von Fotografen mit Kultstatus in Szene gesetzt, darunter Nick Knight, Rankin, Tim Walker, Steve Klein, Miles Aldridge und Roberto Aguilar.

Paddys Arbeiten wurden in Ausstellungen in Grossbritannien, Europa, den USA und Australien vorgestellt und seine Werke finden sich in den Dauerausstellungen der Wellcome Collection (London), des Museum of Arts and Design (New York), dem National Museum of Art, Architecture and Design (Norwegen) und dem National Army Museum (London). Als Gastprofessor hielt er Vorlesungen zu seiner Arbeit an Universitäten und Kunstinstitutionen in Grossbritannien, der EU, Australien und den USA. Besonders hervorzuheben sind seine Präsentationen am V&A (London), KODE (Bergen), dem Science Museum (London), Wellcome Trust (London) und dem Museum of Arts and Design (New York).

Im November 2015 wurde die Ausstellung «Papaver Rhoeas» an 11 Standorten in London eröffnet. Diese Ausstellung umfasste eine Serie von naturgetreuen Mohnblumen, die vollständig aus Lammherz-Gewebe hergestellt waren. Jede einzelne Blume war als pathologisches Präparat in massgefertigten, mundgeblasenen Patronenhülsen aus Glas in Wasser konserviert. Als ergreifendes Symbol des Verlusts von Leben im Krieg und dem unausweichlichen Verlust des Gedächtnisses verfielen diese Mohnblumen nach und nach oder lösten sich — transparenter werdend — auf. «Papaver Rhoeas» wurde im Rahmen der Britischen Feierlichkeiten zum Ersten Weltkrieg bis Ende 2018 an verschiedenen Orten in Grossbritannien gezeigt.

Heute lebt und arbeitet Paddy in Berwick-upon-Tweed, England. Er stammt ursprünglich aus Dewsbury in West Yorkshire und ist ein Absolvent des University of Wales Institute mit einem Masterabschluss in Bildhauerei und Keramik.

Paddy Hartley: Biography

Commissioned by Roche in 2020, 'The Cost of Life' is Paddy's first exhibition in ceramics, and also his first retrospective.

Paddy Hartley's work is internationally exhibited, collected and published. His artistic practice investigates themes including memorialisation and remembrance. He has also interpreted the discourse between faith groups and biomedical research, the ethics of human cloning, and steroid use and abuse in the bodybuilding community. He works in media as diverse as biotissue manipulation and assembly, digital photography, digital embroidery, installation, and garment assemblage, as well as ceramics.

Paddy has held positions as a Visiting Senior Research Fellow in the Department of Tissue Engineering & Biophotonics at King's College London and as Artist in Residence at the National Maritime Museum, London. Much of Paddy's work has been created with the support of the Wellcome Trust. Resulting projects have realised outcomes including the design and creation of his appearance-altering 'Face Corsets', the production of bioglass facial implants for clinical use, and his interpretations for 'Project Facade' — a response to the surgical and personal stories of facially injured World War I servicemen. A study of this work — *Paddy Hartley: Of Faces and Facades* by David Houston Jones and Marjorie Gehrhardt — appeared from Black Dog Publishing (London) in 2015.

Paddy has worked in close collaboration with science and curatorial innovators including Bioglass/Biomaterials Scientist Dr Ian Thompson, King's College London (KCL); Dr Andrew Bamji, the former Gillies Archive Curator; William Edwards, Curator of the Gordon Museum at KCL; and Professor Malcolm Logan at the Randall Division of Cell and Molecular Biophysics, KCL.

Paddy has also designed bespoke face corsets and neckwear for private clients including Lady Gaga, Rihanna, Noomi Rapace, Elizabeth Banks, Georgia May Jagger, Richard Sawdon Smith, Simon Foxton, Edward Enninful, Jacob K and Jonathan Kaye, to name but a few. His designs have been showcased in leading fashion publications including *AnOther Magazine, Vogue Italia/China/Germany/Turkey, V Magazine, W Magazine, Interview, The Hunger* and *Harpers China*. His work has been shot by iconic fashion photographers including Nick Knight, Rankin, Tim Walker, Steve Klein, Miles Aldridge and Roberto Aguilar.

Paddy's work has been exhibited at venues throughout the UK, Europe, the USA and Australia, and his work has been acquired for the permanent collections of the Wellcome Collection (London), the Museum of Arts and Design (New York), the National Museum of Art, Architecture and Design (Norway) and the National Army Museum (London). As a guest speaker, he has lectured extensively on his practice at universities and arts venues across the UK and additionally throughout the European Union, Australia and the USA. Most notably he has presented at the Victoria & Albert Museum (London), KODE (Bergen), the Science Museum (London), the Wellcome Trust (London) and the Museum of Arts and Design (New York).

November 2015 saw the launch of the exhibition 'Papaver Rhoeas' across 11 venues in central London. This exhibition comprised a series of botanically accurate poppies created entirely from lamb's-heart tissue. Each specimen was preserved as a pathological specimen in custom-made, blown-glass artillery shell casings. In a poignant symbol of the loss of life in war and the inevitable decay of memory, these poppies gradually disintegrated or became virtually transparent over time. 'Papaver Rhoeas' toured venues throughout the UK until the end of 2018, as part of Britain's wider commemoration of World War I.

Now resident in Berwick-upon-Tweed, England, Paddy originates from Dewsbury, West Yorkshire. He is a graduate of the University of Wales Institute, Cardiff, with a Master's Degree in Sculpture and Ceramics.

Paddy Hartley: Ein Künstler zu Hause

Ein höflicher, liebenswerter Mann der leisen Worte, der in unglaublichen Mengen dunkler grauer Wolle und Flausch beinahe versinkt: Dies war mein erster Eindruck von Paddy Hartley, als wir über Google Meet im Januar 2021 erstmals miteinander sprachen. Zur Vorbereitung dieser ersten Begegnung habe ich sowohl das Dokument, welches ich von Alexander Bieri, Kurator des Historischen Archivs Roche erhalten hatte, wie auch den Projektvorschlag, den Paddy Roche im Jahr zuvor vorgelegt hatte, gelesen. Diese Unterlagen bildeten eine Zusammenfassung über die Inspiration zu «The Cost of Life», das Ziel des Projekts und die Herangehensweise, nebst ersten Beschreibungen der geplanten Kunstwerke. Obwohl ich diese Dokumente sorgfältig studierte, hatte ich Mühe, das Wesen des Projekts, über das ich schreiben sollte, zu erfassen. Was war «The Cost of Life»? Ganz klar etwas anderes als Lebenshaltungskosten, aber was war die Essenz dieser Idee? Sicherlich würde ein wichtiger Teil meiner Aufgabe werden, diese Essenz zu verstehen und in Worte zu fassen.

Diese Texte, welche ich las, waren natürlich konzeptioneller und nicht dokumentarischer Natur. Sie behandeln die geplanten Ideen, nicht die entstandenen Kunstwerke. Während der nächsten sechs Monate wurden diese Ideen immer wie konkreter und subtil verfeinert, an gewissen Stellen auch bewusst von Paddy verändert, um seine Erfahrungen bei der Herstellung dieser einzigartigen und enorm ambitionierten Werkgruppe zu spiegeln. Das Werk entwickelte sich über einen kontinuierlichen Dialog zwischen Paddy, seiner Materie und seinen Materialien.

«Es war ein Essay in Keramik über die Patientenerfahrung»

Paddy Hartley: An Artist at Home

A courteous, amiable, soft-spoken figure almost overpowered by improbable quantities of dark grey wool and fleece: that was my first impression of Paddy Hartley when we had our introductory conversation on Google Meet in January of 2021. In preparing for this first encounter, I had read the briefing document supplied to me by Alexander Bieri, Curator of the Roche Historical Collection and Archive, as well as the project proposal that Paddy had submitted to Roche the previous year. These materials provided a summary of the inspiration for 'The Cost of Life', its aim, materials and approach, along with preliminary descriptions of the artworks envisaged. Carefully as I read and re-read these documents, however, I still struggled to understand the nature of the project I had been asked to write about. What was 'The Cost of Life'? Clearly something very different from the cost of living, but what was the essence of the idea? For surely, an important part of my task would be to try to understand that essence and render it in words.

I was, of course, looking at texts that were conceptual rather than documentary. They were about projected ideas, not realised artworks. In the course of the ensuing six months, those ideas were to become far more concrete, subtly refined, and on occasions deliberately altered by Paddy in response to his experience of creating this unique and hugely ambitious suite of artworks. The work evolved by means of a continuous dialogue between Paddy, his subject-matter and his materials.

"It was an essay in ceramics on the experience of the patient"

Sobald die Regelungen zur Ausgangssperre dies erlaubten, habe ich Paddy in seinem Studio in Berwick-upon-Tweed aufgesucht, um aus erster Hand zu erfahren, wie die Konzeption seines Vorschlags für «The Cost of Life» in die dreidimensionale Realität umgesetzt wird und ich begann, langsam zu verstehen, welcher Vorstellung «The Cost of Life» entspringt. Wenn mir die Projektdokumente und Pläne, die ich ursprünglich studiert hatte, komplex erschienen, war die Botschaft der Kunstwerke, die hier im Entstehen begriffen waren, klar. Es war ein Essay in Keramik über die Patientenerfahrung — somit der Erfahrung von uns allen — angesichts der Angst, der Schmerzen und des Leids, aber auch der Hoffnungen und Vorstellungen, die zu der Erfahrung, unsere physischen Körper zu bewohnen, gehören. Krankheit und Verletzung sind ein universeller und unausweichlicher Bestandteil des menschlichen Seins. Wir alle haben mal in irgendeiner Form auf dem Krankenlager gelegen. Wir alle haben unsere Wunden gepflegt. Und wir haben alle diese Erfahrungen bei anderen mitbekommen — Andere, die wir möglicherweise sogar mehr liebhaben, als uns selbst. Paddy bei der Arbeit zu beobachten, führte mir vor Augen, dass er seine Bestimmung als Künstler in höchstem Mass erfüllt: Er teilt uns mit, was wir bereits kennen, aber was wir kaum artikulieren können, weder gegenüber uns selbst noch gegenüber jenen, mit denen wir gerne kommunizieren würden.

Selbst über Google Meet war Paddy ein untadeliger Gastgeber: Immer zur Zeit für die Treffen, immer flexibel, wenn es kurzfristige Änderungen gab und immer zuvorkommend gegenüber meiner Bedürfnisse, selbst wenn er aufgrund seines enorm anspruchsvollen Auftrags unter Druck war. Er war dem Bild des getriebenen Künstlers oder des *enfant terrible* diametral entgegengesetzt, ohne sich je zu beschweren und ohne jedes theatralische Gehabe, selbst wenn die Anstrengung, Tonklumpen von über 7 Kilogramm Gewicht auf der Töpferscheibe zu zentrieren, seine Schulter derart in Mitleidenschaft gezogen hatte, dass er sie über Wochen schienen musste.

«Es ist ein Ort, wo immer wieder klar Schiff gemacht werden muss»

Visiting Paddy in his studio in Berwick-upon-Tweed as soon as lockdown regulations permitted, I was able to observe at first hand how the concept of the proposal for 'The Cost of Life' was being translated into three-dimensional reality, and I gradually began to understand the notion of 'The Cost of Life'. If the proposal and plans that I had originally studied had appeared complex to me, the message of the artworks, even while still in a nascent state, was clear. It was an essay in ceramics on the experience of the patient — that is to say, the experience of us all — in the face of the fear, pain and suffering but also the hopes and imaginings that accompany our experience of inhabiting our physical bodies. Illness and injury are a universal and inescapable part of the human condition. We have all lain on a sick-bed of some kind. We have all nursed some wound or other. And we have all witnessed those experiences in others — others whom we love perhaps even more dearly than we love ourselves. Watching Paddy at work, I realised that he was fulfilling his calling as an artist to the highest degree: he was telling us what we already know, but what we struggle to articulate, either to ourselves or to those with whom we long to be able to speak.

Even on Google Meet, Paddy was an impeccable host: always on time for meetings, always flexible when arrangements had to be changed at short notice, and always considerate of my needs, even when feeling the pressure of this immensely demanding assignment. He was the diametrical opposite of the tortured artist or enfant terrible, with no complaints and no histrionics, even when the effort of throwing pieces of clay weighting in excess of 7 kilograms caused an injury to his right shoulder that required strapping for weeks.

"It is a place where the decks have to be cleared time and time and time again"

Als ich zusammen mit dem Filmemacher Barry Gibb sein Studio in Berwick-upon-Tweed besuchte, um eine Reihe von Dokumentarfilmen über Paddy bei der Arbeit an «The Cost of Life» zu drehen, fiel mir sofort die friedliche Atmosphäre in Paddy's Studio auf, eine Atmosphäre, die von der akribischen Ordnung der Werkzeuge und der Materialien ausgeht, von der sorgsamen Platzierung der sowohl vollendeten wie auch der in Entstehung befindlichen Kunstwerke und der Gegenwart seiner geliebten getigerten Katze, die er Mrs Phoons getauft hat. Dieser Ort muss peinlich sauber und aufgeräumt gehalten werden, da die Beschaffenheit der Materialien, mit denen Paddy arbeitet, dies erfordert und auch, um die Gefahr der Kreuz-Kontamination auszuschliessen. Es ist ebenso ein Ort, wo immer wieder klar Schiff gemacht werden muss, um den physischen und geistigen Rahmen zu schaffen, der für komplexe und ambitionierte Arbeiten notwendig ist.

Als ich Paddy bei der Arbeit zusah, war ich von der Kombination aus Kraft und Sensibilität beeindruckt, die jede seiner Bewegungen beeinflusst. Er ist kräftig gebaut und verfügt über enorme körperliche Energie, aber seine Finger sind äusserst zartfühlend und sein Auge präzise und scharf. Anstrengende Phasen an der Töpferscheibe, die ungewöhnlich grosse und schwere Tonbrocken beinhalten, wechseln sich mit penibler kleinteiliger und zeitaufwendiger Arbeit ab. Und immer wieder experimentiert er mit neuen Techniken, wodurch er die Grenzen des Möglichen auslotet, halb vermutend, halb erfühlend, wie er seine Konzeption in die Realität umsetzen kann.

Barry und ich besuchten Paddy zwei Mal während des Projekts — einmal in sehr kaltem Wetter mit Temperaturen nahe des Gefrierpunkts und ein anderes Mal, als es mild und warm war. Wir erlebten Berwick-upon-Tweed von beiden Seiten: Verriegelt, düster und vom Nordsee-Wind gebeutelt und dann andererseits von der Sonne beglückt und träge unter dem weiten Himmel der Küste. Trotz des Drucks seiner Arbeit — und er arbeitete oftmals bis nach Mitternacht, um dann frühmorgens wieder mit der Arbeit zu beginnen — blieb Paddy ein unfehlbar aufmerksamer und grosszügiger Gastgeber, stets auf den Komfort und das Wohlbefinden seiner Gäste bedacht. Zudem ist er ein immer verlässlicher, guter Gefährte und ein geistreicher Erzähler. Barry und ich haben beide ein Zuhause fernab des eigenen Heims in Berwick-upon-Tweed gefunden, welches uns unvergesslich bleiben wird.

«Es ist offensichtlich, dass er mit seinen Ideen und seinen Materialien völlig im Einklang ist»

Visiting his studio in Berwick-upon-Tweed together with the film-maker Barry James Gibb to make a series of documentary films about Paddy at work on 'The Cost of Life', I was immediately struck by the atmosphere of peace that prevailed in Paddy's studio, an atmosphere conveyed by the meticulous ordering of his equipment and materials, the thoughtful placement of his artworks, both completed and in progress, and the presence of his beloved cat, a tortoiseshell tabby named Mrs Phoons. This is a place that has to be kept meticulously clean and tidy on account of the nature of the materials Paddy uses for his work and the danger of cross-contamination between them. It is also a place where the decks have to be cleared time and time and time again to create the physical and also the mental space for working on complex and ambitious builds.

Watching Paddy work, I was impressed by the combination of strength and sensitivity that informed his every movement. He is powerfully built, with tremendous energy in his body, but his fingers are capable of extraordinary delicacy, and his eye is like a gimlet. Intense sessions of throwing on the wheel, involving extremely large and heavy pieces of clay, alternate with painstakingly fine and time-consuming work. And time and again, he is experimenting with new techniques, testing the boundaries of the possible, half-guessing and half-feeling his way towards the realisation of his conception.

Barry and I visited Paddy twice during the course of the project — once in conditions that were near-freezing and once in conditions that were balmy and warm. We experienced Berwick-upon-Tweed from both its sides: shuttered and dour and lashed by the winds from the North Sea, and then again, basking languorously under towering blue maritime skies. Despite the pressure of his work — and he was frequently working into the small hours, to resume work again early the following morning — Paddy remained an unfailingly thoughtful and generous host, anxious for the comfort and well-being of his guests, as well as being a perennially good companion and witty raconteur. Barry and I both found a little bit of home in Berwick-upon-Tweed that will always stay with us.

"It is clear that he is entirely at home with his ideas and his materials"

Während unserer zahlreichen Gespräche, zunächst online und danach von Angesicht zu Angesicht, hat Paddy oft darauf hingewiesen, wie wichtig es für ihn war, dieses neue Zuhause zu finden, das ihm erlaubt, ohne Beschränkungen genau so zu arbeiten, wie er immer wollte. Als ich ihn über längere Zeit beobachten konnte, wurde offensichtlich, dass er mit seinen Ideen und seinen Materialien völlig im Einklang ist, so herausfordernd sie sich auch herausstellen mögen; er erwähnt oftmals die Bedeutung des Scheiterns im Prozess der Herstellung vollendeter Kunstwerke. Er ist in seinem Studio zu Hause, er ist in seiner Wahlheimat zu Hause und – überhaupt am Wichtigsten – er ist vollkommen in sich selbst zu Hause. Nachdem ich das Privileg hatte, dem Entstehungsprozess dieser aussergewöhnlichen Werkgruppe beizuwohnen, werden nun viele Menschen die Möglichkeit bekommen, sich mit ihr und den Gedanken, die sie auslöst, auseinanderzusetzen und ich hoffe auch, dass Paddy in den kommenden Jahren viele weitere zum Nachdenken anregende Kunstwerke schaffen wird. Ich bin sicher, dass er dies tun wird.

During the course of our many conversations, initially online and then face to face, Paddy often emphasized the importance to him of finding this new home, which allows him full rein to work as he has always wanted to. Observing him over a long period of time, it is clear that he is entirely at home with his ideas and his materials, however challenging these might prove; he makes frequent mention of the importance of failures in the process of creating finished artworks. He is at home in his studio, at home in his chosen city, and, most important of all, at home in himself.

Having had the privilege of witnessing the genesis of this extraordinary suite of artworks, I hope that many people will have the opportunity to engage with them and the thoughts they encourage, and I hope too that Paddy will produce many more thought-provoking works of art in the years to come. I am sure he will.

Berwick →

Basel

The Cost of Life

Veranstaltungsort
· The Venue

DAS MUSEUM TINGUELY wurde 1996 aus Anlass des 100. Jubiläums von Roche eingeweiht. Bis heute stellt es das bedeutendste Kulturengagement von Roche dar, das Museum wird vollständig vom Unternehmen getragen. Die Sammlung mit Werken des kinetischen Künstlers Jean Tinguely entstand zunächst aus Schenkungen der Roche-Aktionäre Maja und Paul Sacher, der Witwe des Künstlers Niki de Saint-Phalle und von Roche. Seit der Eröffnung ist das Museum Tinguely dank seines anspruchsvollen und über die vergangenen 25 Jahre beständig entwickelten Ausstellungsprogramms zu einem Zentrum für kinetische Kunst geworden. Die Idee dazu ist von Paul Sacher ausgegangen, der damit auch das Engagement seiner verstorbenen Frau Maja, die mit Jean Tinguely befreundet war, würdigen wollte. Gleichzeitig ergab sich durch das Projekt die Möglichkeit, den an Roche Basel angrenzenden Solitude-Park aufzuwerten. Mario Botta schuf dafür ein Bauwerk, das sich gegen den Park öffnet und diesen von der Autobahn abschirmt. Im Museum, dem Park und den Restaurants vermischen sich heute Gäste des Museums mit Anwohnern und Mitarbeitenden von Roche, womit ein wertvoller Ort des Austausches und der Erholung entstanden ist.

THE MUSEUM TINGUELY was opened to the public in 1996 as part of the 100 year jubilee of Roche. Until today, it is the most significant single cultural commitment of Roche and the museum is fully supported by contributions of the company. Its collection of works by Swiss kinetic artist Jean Tinguely comprises donations by the former main shareholders of Roche Maja and Paul Sacher, the artist's widow Niki de Saint-Phalle and also of Roche. Thanks to its ambitious exhibition programme which has been continuously developed during the past 25 years, the Museum Tinguely has become a centre of competence for kinetic art. The main proponent of the idea was Paul Sacher, thereby honouring the dedication of his late wife Maja who had been a close friend of Jean Tinguely. Concurrently, the project offered an opportunity to upgrade the Solitude park which adjoins the headquarters of Roche Basel. The architect Mario Botta designed a building that opens on the park and shields it from the motorway running next to it. Today, visitors of the museum, local residents and Roche employees mingle in the museum, the park and its restaurants, making it a valuable place for exchange and recreation.

You Can Have Any Colour As Long as it's Blue

Die Konzeption des Werks

Diese Arbeit behandelt den Erfolg der «in-vitro-Fertilisation» (IVF) und das Potential der Genom-Editierung. Der Titel bezieht sich auf die berühmte Äusserung des Amerikanischen Industriellen Henry Ford, Gründer der Ford Motor Company, der wesentlich an der Erfindung des Fliessbands beteiligt war, auf der die Massenproduktion beruht.

IVF hat über die Jahre hinweg enorme Forschritte gemacht. 1978 wurde das erste mittels IVF gezeugte Kind, Louise Brown, geboren. Bis 2018 führten die Verbesserungen der IVF-Technologie zu einer durchschnittlichen IVF Geburtsrate von 23% aller Embryos. IVF ist ein sich rasch entwickelnder wissenschaftlicher Bereich, obwohl der Prozess teuer und für die künftigen Eltern herausfordernd ist.

Menschen streben von Natur aus nach Verbesserung, Entdeckung, Verwirklichung und Erforschung. «Ich glaube, dass die Genom-Editierung bei menschlichen Embryos schliesslich allgegenwärtig werden wird», meint Paddy Hartley. «Sie wird zunehmend dazu gebraucht werden, den Zufall bei der Erschaffung des Kindes auszuschalten. Ihr Ziel wird sein, das Traumkind der Eltern herzustellen: Ein Abbild ihrer selbst, nur besser.» Diese Arbeit ist eine Synthese bestehend aus einem Roulette-Rad und einer Laborzentrifuge, ein Gerät, welches die Drehung kontrolliert, um den Zufall auszuschalten.

MEDIUM: Keramik
MASSE: 37 cm Durchmesser, 2 Objekte
JAHR: 2021

You Can Have Any Colour As Long as it's Blue

Imagining the work

This work is about the success of *in vitro* fertilisation (IVF) and the potential of gene editing. The title refers to the famous saying of the American industrialist Henry Ford, founder of the Ford Motor Company and chief developer of the assembly line technique of mass production.

IVF has made huge advances over the years. The first IVF birth was Louise Brown, who was born in 1978. By 2018, improvements in IVF technology had taken the average IVF birth rate per embryo transferred to 23%. IVF is an area of science which is improving rapidly, although the process remains expensive and highly challenging for the would-be parents.

Humans by their nature seek to improve, discover, achieve and explore. "I believe that gene editing in human embryos will eventually become commonplace" observes Paddy Hartley. "It will be increasingly used to eliminate the element of chance in the creation of the child. Its aim will be to produce a child the parents' dream of: an image of themselves, only better." This work is a synthesis of a roulette wheel and a laboratory centrifuge, a device that controls the outcome of the spin so as to remove the element of chance.

MEDIA: Ceramic
DIMENSIONS: 37 cm diameter, 2 objects

DATE: 2021

Herstellungsprozess

Diese Arbeiten wurden vollständig auf der Töpferscheibe geschaffen. Sie umfassen mehrere grosse, auf der Scheibe gedrehte Komponenten, die innen hohl und röhrenartig aufgebaut sind, und so die Kugelbahn und die obere Einbuchtung des Roulette-Rads bilden. Diese Teile umschliessen einen kleinen, zentralen Drehteller, der seinerseits aus einer einzigen, auf der Scheibe geschaffenen, Form mit hohlen Bereichen besteht.

Die Einbuchtungen für die Kugel sind so gestaltet, dass jede Drehung des Rads ein wiederholtes, kontrolliertes Resultat erzielen soll. Die blaue Iris des Auges und verschiedene Blautöne sind die hauptsächlich zur Auswahl stehenden Variationen, doch ist der Zufall durch die einzige bestimmte Farbvariation immer noch präsent. Die Zufälligkeit ist also ausgeschaltet, aber eben doch nicht ganz. Obwohl das Werk sofort als Roulette-Rad erkennbar ist, lässt es doch auch an eine Zentrifuge denken, denn Details daran sind an die Ästhetik von Zentrifugen angelehnt. Die logische Konsequenz der Genom-Editierung ist, ein kontrolliertes Resultat zu erzielen — welches aus Sicht derjenigen, die diesen Prozess beeinflussen, erwünscht ist.

«Die logische Konsequenz der Genom-Editierung ist, ein kontrolliertes Resultat zu erzielen — welches in den Augen derjenigen, die den Prozess kontrollieren, erwünscht ist.»

Building the work

Built entirely on the potter's wheel, these works comprise multiple large, thrown components which are circular, hollow and tubular in shape, equating to the ball track and recesses of a roulette wheel. These are positioned around a central spinning section which is likewise a single, thrown form with hollow sections.

The ball recesses are loaded with a series of outcome variations which are based on achieving a repeated, controlled outcome of each spin of the wheel. The coloured iris of the eye in blue and variations of blue is the predominant outcome offered, yet the element of chance is still present in the form of a single distinct colour variation. Chance is eliminated, but not entirely. While immediately recognisable as a roulette wheel, this piece also suggests a centrifuge, with details of the wheel evoking the visual aesthetic of centrifuges. The logical consequence of gene editing is to create an outcome that is controlled — and desirable in the eye of whoever is controlling the process.

"The logical consequence of gene editing is to create an outcome that is controlled — and desirable in the eye of whoever is controlling the process."

The End… to be continued

Die Konzeption des Werks

Diese Arbeit lotet Haltungen gegenüber der medizinischen Behandlung am Lebensende sowie der Euthanasie aus. Sie besteht aus Begräbnisurnen, die mit Injektionskanülen versehen sind. Die Urnen können weder in die Hand genommen noch umarmt werden. Der Tod kann nicht dauerhaft ferngehalten werden, selbst nicht mit medizinischen Mitteln. Die Eingebung für dieses Werk kam Paddy während der COVID-19 Pandemie, als Krankenhäuser äusserst schmerzliche Besuchsrestriktionen verhängten. «Nicht alle verstehen, dass Menschen 'bereit für den Tod' sein können,» reflektiert er. «Viele haben mit dieser Vorstellung Mühe.» Paddy sieht die Verlängerung des Lebens bis hin zu einer Existenz des Leidens als eine Art Missbrauch. «Wir entscheiden uns nicht, geboren zu werden,» sagt er: «Wir sollten zumindest entscheiden dürfen, wann wir sterben.»

MEDIUM: Keramik, Kanülen
MASSE: 7 Urnen, Höhe zwischen 23–27 cm, 13 Urnen ohne Nadeln Höhe zwischen 18–21 cm
JAHR: 2021

The End... to be continued

Imagining the work

This work explores attitudes towards end-of-life medical treatments and euthanasia. It presents funeral urns embellished with cannula needles. The urns cannot be held; they cannot be embraced. Death cannot be staved off, even by medical interventions. The idea for this piece came to Paddy during the COVID-19 pandemic, when hospital visiting restrictions were at their most brutal. "Not everyone understands that people can be 'ready to die'," he reflects. "Many struggle to accept this notion." Paddy regards the prolongation of life into an existence of suffering as a form of abuse. "We do not choose to be born," he says: "We should at least be able to choose when we die."

MEDIA: Ceramic, piercing needles
DIMENSIONS: 7 urns, height between 23–27 cm, 13 urns without needles height between 18–21 cm

DATE: 2021

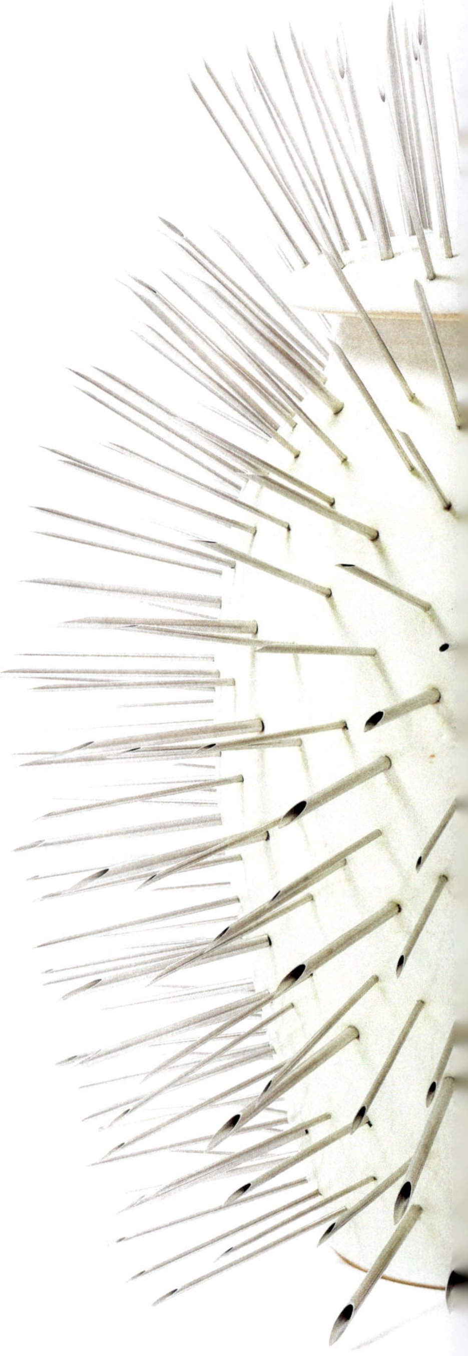

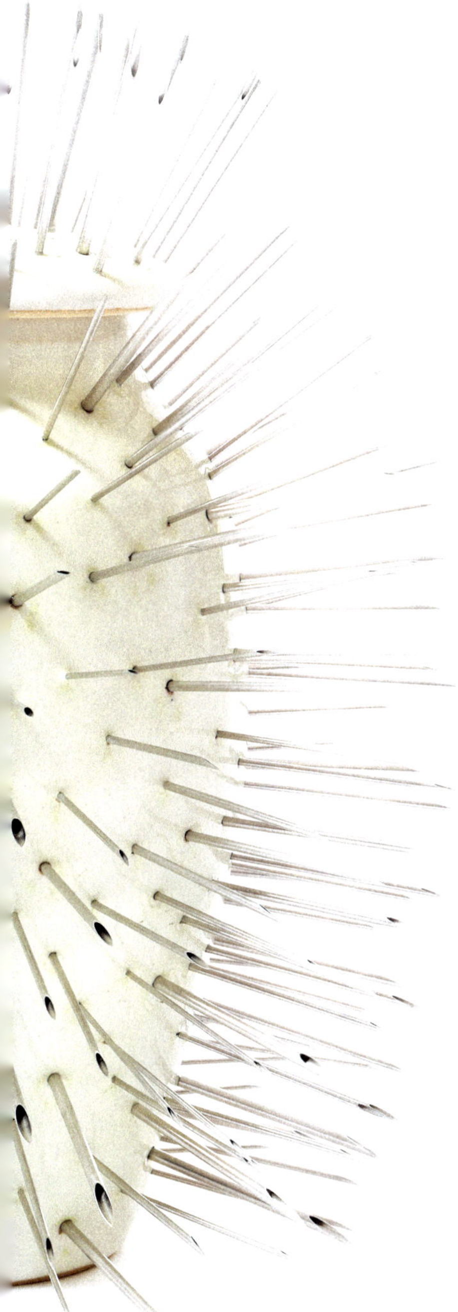

«Nicht alle akzeptieren, dass Menschen ‹bereit für den Tod› sein können. Viele haben mit dieser Vorstellung Mühe.»

Herstellungsprozess

«Was ich mir vorstelle, wenn ich Dinge schaffe, hat einen unmittelbaren Einfluss auf die Arbeit in meinen Händen,» sagt Paddy. «Wie ich mit dem Ton umgehe. Wie ich die Glasur behandle. Wie ich die Glasur auftrage. Wie ich das Werk brenne. Meine Arbeit entwickelt sich unaufhörlich auf jeder Stufe des Gestehungsprozesses und selbst dann, wenn die Arbeit vollendet ist. Die Gruppierung und Aufstellung der einzelnen Werke sind auch ein Bestandteil der Gesamtkomposition.»

Paddy beschreibt die Begräbnisurnen als das am Häufigsten wiederaufgegriffene Projekt dieses Auftrags, wenn es um den Herstellungsprozess geht. Nachdem er 30 Varianten aufgebaut hatte, entschied er sich dazu, dass sich alle sehr ähnlich sein sollten, um die Ähnlichkeit des Dilemmas auszudrücken, dem sich alle in solch einer Situation gegenübersehen. Doch ist jede Urne nichtsdestotrotz in Form, Grösse und Oberfläche subtil differenziert gestaltet, wodurch zum Ausdruck kommt, dass wir alle gleichzeitig ähnlich und anders sind.

Jedes auf der Scheibe gedrehte Gefäss ist mit einer Matrix aus Einstichstellen mit Kanülen versehen, wobei einige mit Absicht strukturiert und geordnet gesetzt erscheinen, andere zufällig und chaotisch. Die Nadeln verunmöglichen es beinahe vollständig, die Urnen in der Hand zu halten und verfärben zudem die Glasur, was den Eindruck der hilflosen Pein symbolisiert, welche die Erfahrung des Kontrollentzugs über das eigene Sterben beflecken kann. Diese bearbeiteten Urnen sind zwischen nadellosen Urnen verteilt, in Anerkennung der Tatsache, dass verzögertes oder kontrolliertes Sterben nicht der Erfahrung Aller entspricht, unabhängig davon, ob man sich bewusst dazu entschieden hat oder der Tod zufällig eingetreten ist.

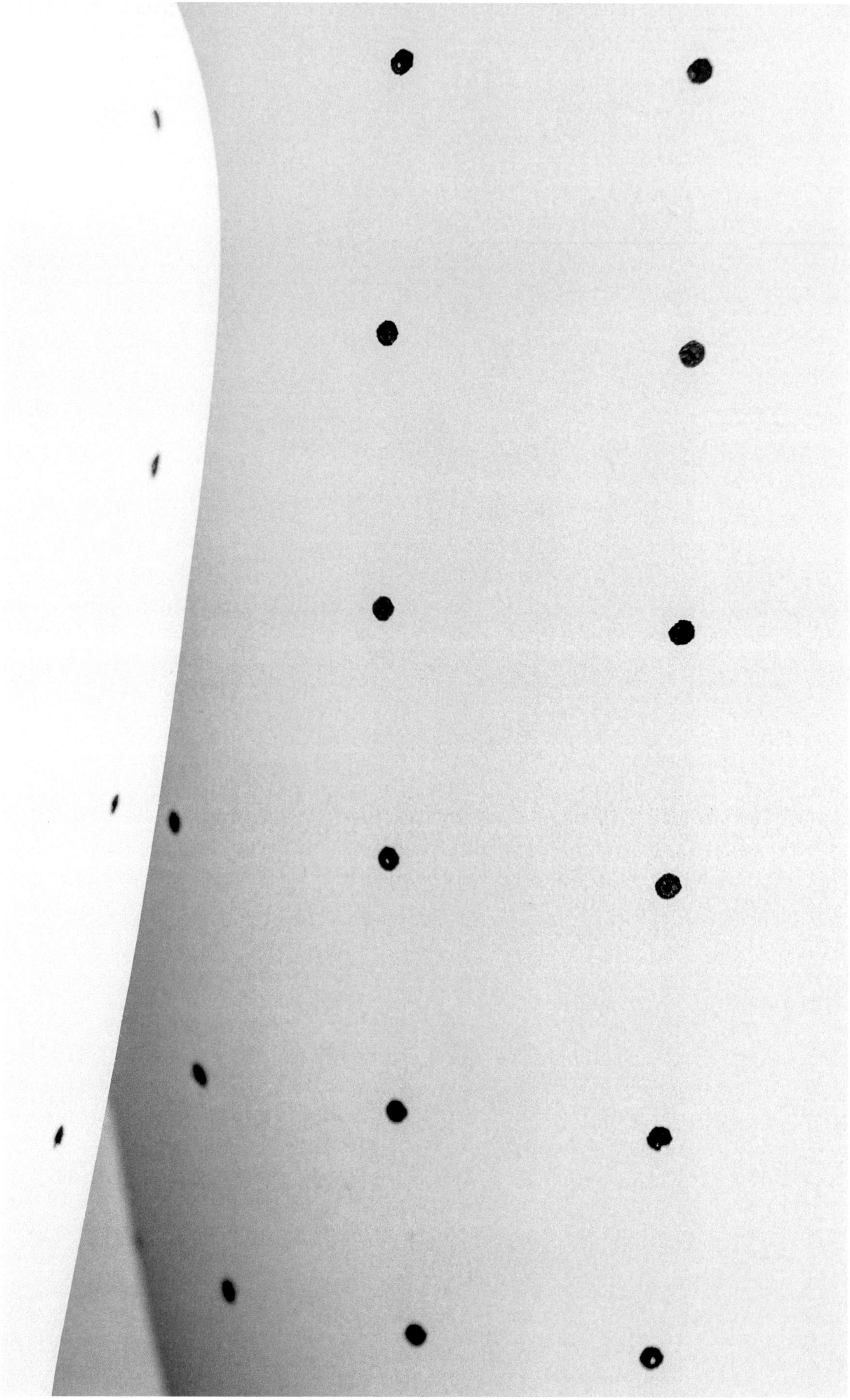

Building the work

"What I'm thinking about as I make has a direct impact on the work in my hands," says Paddy. "How I treat the clay. How I treat the glaze. How I apply the glaze. How I fire the work. My work is constantly evolving through each stage of the make, and even after the make is complete. The grouping and presentation of the individual works are also intrinsic to the overall work."

Paddy describes the funeral urns as the most revisited of the works in this collection in terms of the making process. After initially building 30 variants, he decided to make them all very similar, to express the similar nature of the quandary faced by people in this situation. Each urn has subtle variations in form, scale and surface, acknowledging that we are all similar and different at the same time.

Each thrown form is punctured with a matrix of cannula needles, some structured and orderly, placed with purpose and intent, others randomly and chaotically. The presence of these needles makes the urn nearly impossible to hold and discolours the glaze, acknowledging the sense of taintedness that can be associated with the dying experience being taken out of the patient's control. These embellished urns are distributed amongst a group of urns devoid of needles, acknowledging the fact that the delayed or controlled dying process is not a process experienced by all, whether by choice or imposition.

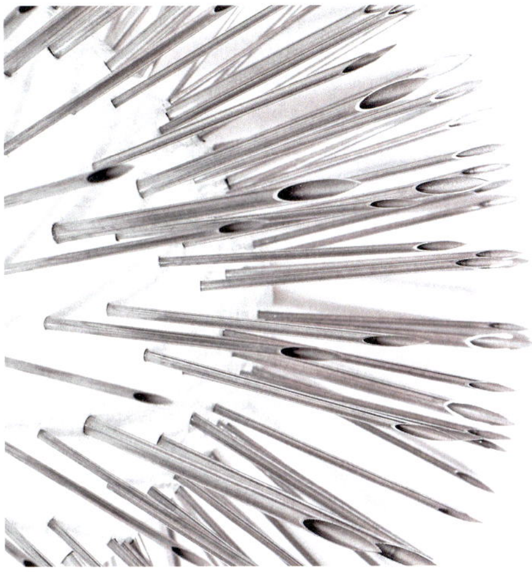

"Not everyone understands that people can be 'ready to die'. Many struggle to accept this notion."

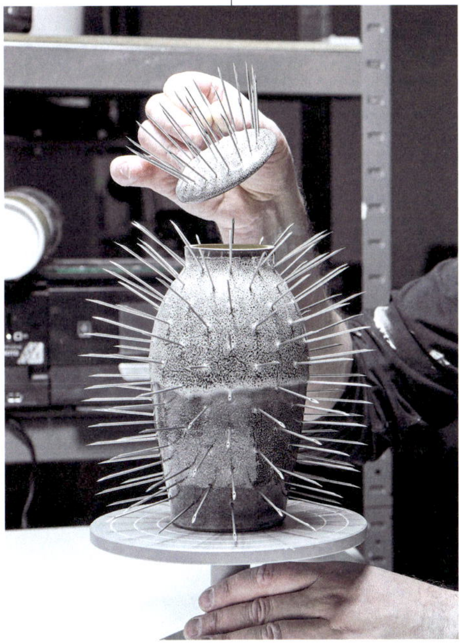

Ill Communication

Die Konzeption des Werks

Diese Arbeit wurde durch den Einfluss des Internets und von Social Media auf die wissenschaftliche Kommunikation inspiriert. Die Popularisierung der Wissenschaft in all ihren Facetten war nie weiter fortgeschritten, als heute und das Internet hat eine enorme Rolle dabei gespielt, Zugang zu Wissenschaft und Lehre zu ermöglichen. Die Kehrseite davon ist die absichtliche Fehlinterpretation wissenschaftlicher und medizinischer Aspekte durch einzelne Akteure. Dadurch wird die Verbreitung korrekter Wissenschaft und der daraus resultierenden Fortschritte erschwert.

Das Internet ist als kommunikatives Medium ein zweischneidiges Schwert, da es Informationen ohne Differenzierung zwischen «guter» oder «schlechter» Information verbreitet. Die Gestaltung der Ill Communication Dishes vermittelt genau diese Verbreitung toxischer Informationen — unter Anwendung von strukturierter Effizienz.

MEDIUM: Keramik
MASSE: 36–55 cm Durchmesser, 8 Objekte
JAHR: 2021

Ill Communication

Imagining the work

This work is inspired by the impact of the internet and social media on science communication. The popularisation of science in all its forms has never been greater, and the internet has played an enormous part in giving people access to science and to science education at all levels. The drawback of this is that the deliberate misrepresentation of some aspects of science and medicine by certain individuals and groups makes it more challenging to disseminate accurate science and to make its benefits available to the world at large.

The internet as a communication tool is a double-edged sword, disseminating 'good' information and allowing the spread of 'bad' information at the same time. The Ill Communication Dishes are designed to convey the spread of toxic information — with a structured efficiency.

MEDIA: Ceramic
DIMENSIONS: 36–55 cm diameter, 8 objects

DATE: 2021

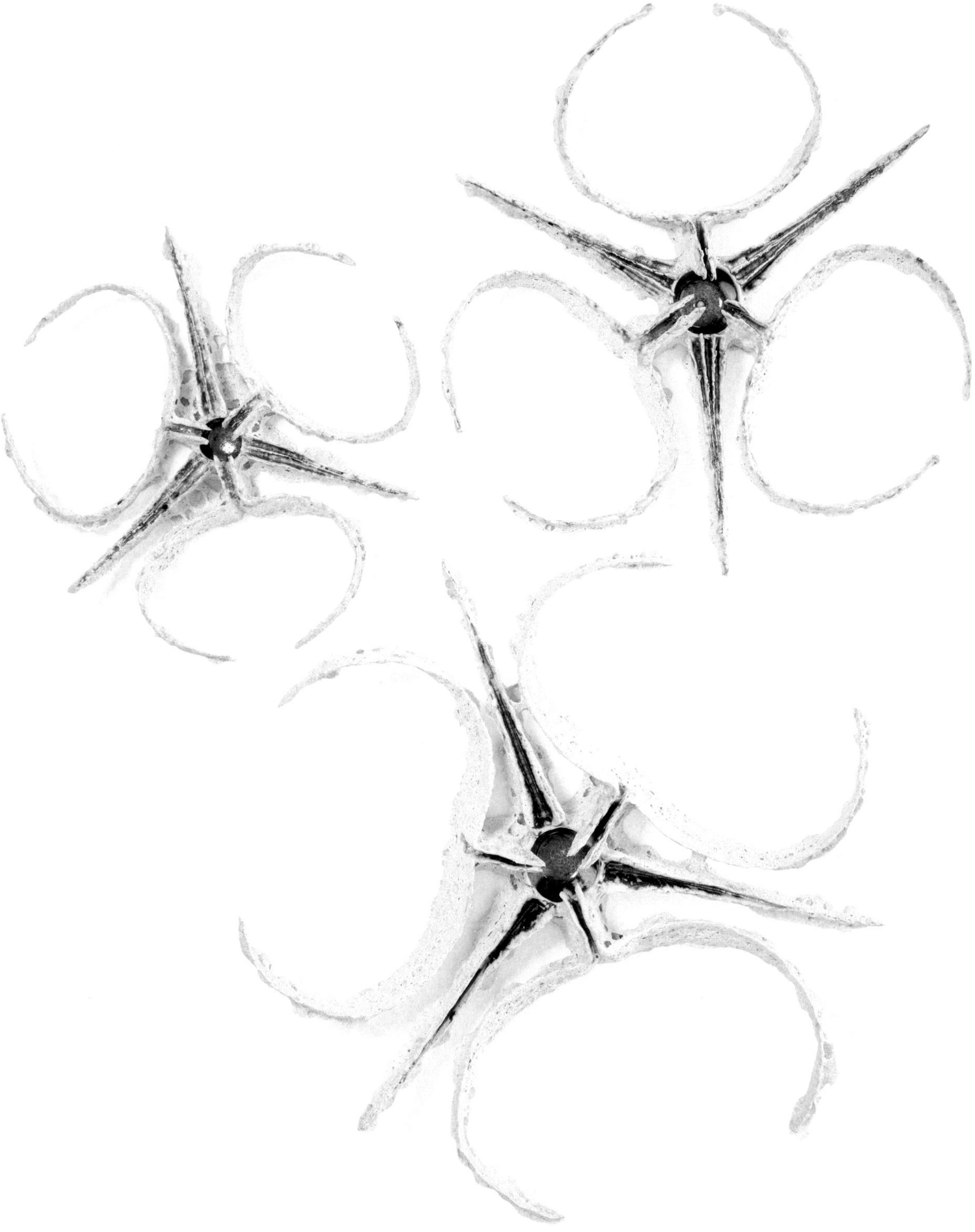

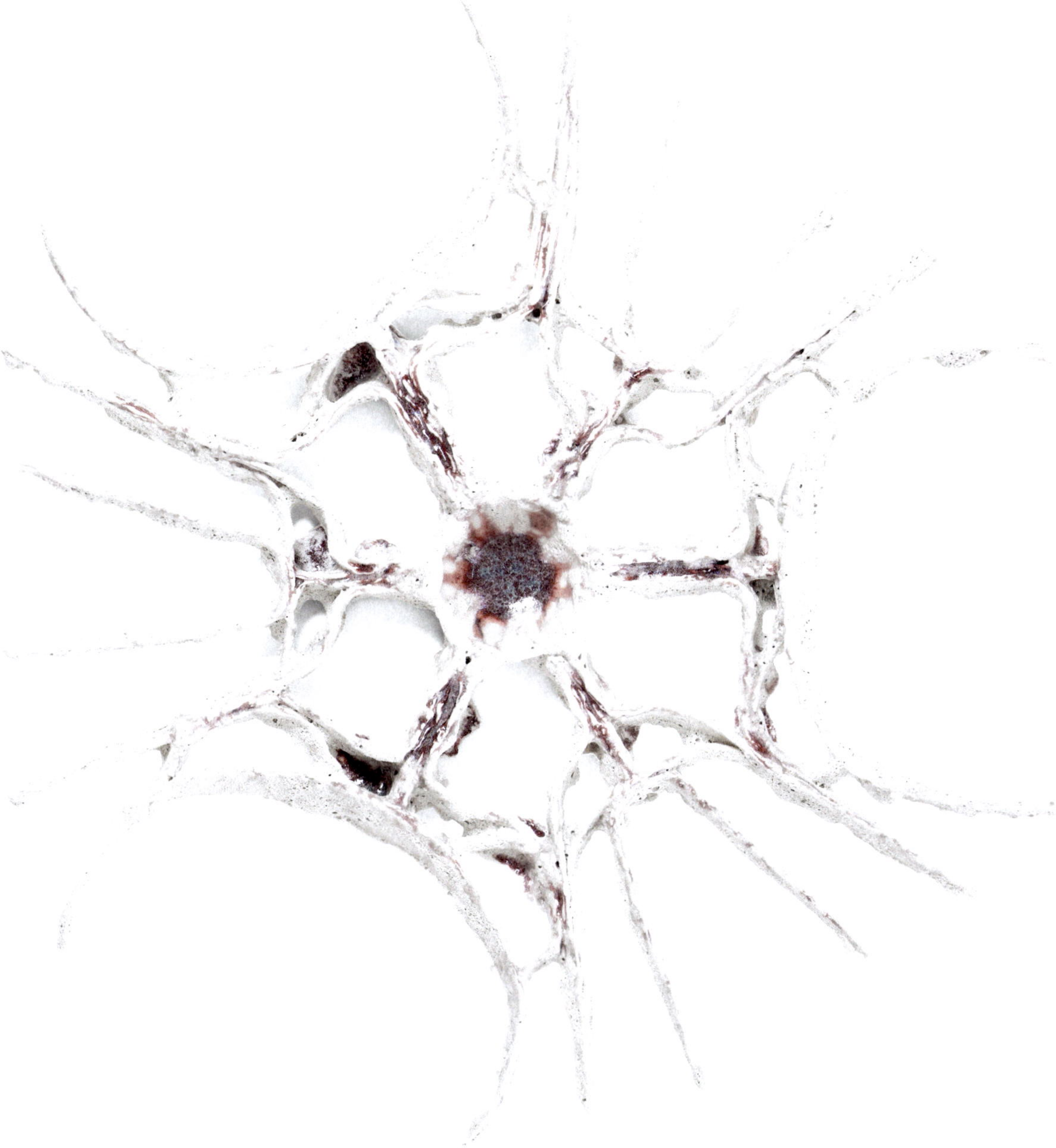

«Die Ill Communication Dishes sind zur Verbreitung toxischer Informationen gestaltet — und tun dies sehr effizient.»

Herstellungsprozess

Als Paddy die Grundlagen für dieses Werk während der COVID-19 Pandemie erarbeitete, wurde in den Medien regelmässig die R-Zahl verbreitet. Die R-Zahl bezieht sich auf die Anzahl der Menschen, die ihrerseits von einer infizierten Person im Durchschnitt angesteckt werden. Damals lag die R-Rate von COVID-19 bei 3. Paddy dachte andauernd über dieses 1:3 Verhältnis nach. «Ich sehe eine gewisse Schönheit in der Effizienz, mit der sich Viren verbreiten,» reflektiert er. «Falschinformation werden über Social Media ganz ähnlich weiterverbreitet.»

Während er über mögliche Symbole nachdachte, die er in dieser Arbeit verwenden könnte, orientierte sich Paddy an den Piktogrammen auf einigen der digitalen Geräte, die er benutzt — spezifisch dem USB-Symbol, dem Zeichen für das Wi-Fi Signal und parallel dazu dem Symbol für Biogefahren Alle drei verfügen über eine dreigeteilte Struktur, die sich in der Komposition der Ill Communication Dishes spiegelt, die ihrerseits an Satellitenschüsseln erinnern. Die Äste der Schüsselformen wurden in einer Technik hergestellt, bei der Ton mit den Daumen und Fingerspitzen verteilt wird, um ultradünne Flächen herzustellen. Nachdem diese in den grossen Schüsselformen zusammengesetzt worden sind, werden sie darin mit Aluminiumhydroxidsand bedeckt, um das Risiko von Verformungen während des Hochtemperaturbrands zu reduzieren.

Eine Lavaglasur, organisch in ihrer Erscheinung und im Brand notorisch flüssig, bedeckt die Arme der Schüsselformen, selektiv wurden darauf zusätzlich reaktive Glasuren aufgebracht. Die Schüsseln werden dann in einem Korb aus Keramikfaser gebrannt, der flüssige Glasur auffängt und vom Werkstück fernhält. Anschliessend werden die Keramikfasern abgewaschen, um die fertige Form sowie die Ausblühungen der Glasur freizulegen. Durch diesen aufwendigen Prozess scheint sich die Oberfläche der Glasur sowohl organisch in alle Richtungen wie auch parallel zu verteilen — genau wie die Falschinformationen.

Building the work

When Paddy was conducting research for this work during the COVID-19 pandemic, the R-number was regularly in the news. The R-number refers to the number of people a person infected with a virus is likely to infect in turn. At the time, the R-number for COVID-19 was 3. Paddy was continually thinking about this 1:3 ratio. "There is a certain beauty in the efficiency by which viruses spread," he reflects. "Misinformation spreads via social media in a similar way."

Thinking about symbols he might incorporate into the work, Paddy drew direction from the icons on some of the digital devices he uses — specifically the USB symbol, the Wi-Fi signal symbol and, in parallel, the biohazard symbol. All three have a tripartite structure and are reflected in the composition of the Ill Communication Dishes, which themselves have echoes of satellite dishes. The branches of the Dish forms are created using a technique whereby the clay is spread with the thumbs and fingertips to create ultra-thin sheets of clay. Once assembled in a large dish mould, these are buried in alumina hydrate sand within a ceramic cradle to negate the warping the clay would otherwise undergo at high temperatures.

A lava glaze, organic in appearance and prone to run, is used on the arms of the Dish forms and additionally coated selectively with reactive glazes. The Dishes are then fired in a ceramic fibre cradle that captures the run and spread away from the ceramic form. The ceramic fibre is subsequently washed away to reveal the ceramic form and glaze 'bleed', which has the quality of appearing by design to spread both organically and in parallel — like miscommunication.

"The Ill Communication Dishes are designed to spread toxic information — very efficiently."

Looking Class

Die Konzeption des Werks

Diese Arbeit entstand als Resultat von Paddy Hartleys Überlegungen zu der Besessenheit der Gesellschaft von Schönheitsbehandlungen und der Zweckentfremdung rekonstruktiver Chirurgie durch die Schönheitsindustrie. Obwohl die Themengebiete körperdysmorphe Störungen und invasive Schönheitsbehandlungen anlässlich des Symposiums «The Challenge of Life» 1971 keine Rolle spielten, haben sie sich zu einer ethischen und medizinischen Besorgnis entwickelt. Ein wichtiger Bereich in Paddys früheren Werken ist seine Arbeit zu der Entwicklung der rekonstruktiven Gesichtschirurgie für Britische Veteranen, die im Ersten Weltkrieg Verletzungen erlitten hatten. Ironischerweise waren die Chirurgen, die diese revolutionären Techniken entwikkelt haben — zumindest aus der Sichtweise des Pioniers Sir Harold Gillies — später für die Entstehung der Schönheitschirurgie-Industrie verantwortlich (die von Gillies «Cinderella-Chirurgie» genannt wurde).

Der Einfluss der heutigen milliardenschweren Industrie der kosmetischen Chirurgie, kombiniert mit immer aufdringlicheren Idealisierungen der menschlichen Körperform, lässt Ängste über die von uns bewohnten Körper aufkommen. «Schau in den Spiegel, was siehst Du dann?» fragt Paddy. «Ein Gesicht und ein Körper, die als unvollkommen gelten und all die Qual, die dabei mitschwingt».

MEDIUM: Keramik, schwarzes Glas
MASSE: 52 × 40 × 10 cm, 2 Objekte

JAHR: 2021

Looking Class

Imagining the work

This work is the product of Paddy's reflections on society's obsession with beauty treatments and the misuse of reconstructive surgery techniques by the beauty industry. Although the topics of body dysmorphia, cosmetic surgery and invasive beauty treatments were not addressed by the 'Challenge of Life' symposium of 1971, they have grown to become a topic of ethical and medical concern today. A significant element of Paddy's past portfolio is his work on the development of facial reconstructive surgery for British servicemen injured during World War I. Ironically, the surgeons involved in the development and application of these revolutionary techniques were — in the view the pioneering practitioner Sir Harold Gillies — subsequently responsible for the creation of the 'beauty surgery' industry (or as Gillies termed it, 'Cinderella Surgery').

The influence of today's multi-billion pound cosmetic surgery industry, in combination with ever more insistent idealisations of the human form, has generated burgeoning anxiety about the bodies we inhabit. "Look in the mirror, and what do you see?" asks Paddy. "A face and body that are judged inadequate, and all the pain that goes with that."

MEDIA: Ceramic, black glass
DIMENSIONS: 52 × 40 × 10 cm, 2 objects

DATE: 2021

Herstellungsprozess

Die Skulptur lehnt sich an einen ornamentierten Spiegelrahmen an, der vom Barock oder vom Rokoko inspiriert und von Paddys Interesse an griechischer Mythologie und Medizin beeinflusst ist.

«Ich wollte etwas schaffen, was faszinierend abscheulich aussieht», sagt Paddy. Die Ornamente des Spiegelrahmens sind eine Verschmelzung der Gorgone Medusa – der geflügelten Kreatur, die anstelle von Haaren lebende Schlangen trägt – und einem stielförmigen Hauttransplantat, eine Transplantationstechnik, bei der man einen Hautlappen an einer Stelle mit dem Körper verbunden lässt, während der Hauptteil über dem Bereich befestigt wird, der mit Haut bedeckt werden soll.

Das schlangenartige Haar der Gorgone wird mit stummeligen, Egel-artigen Formen mit Falten, Säumen und zornigen kleinen Mündern dargestellt, die sich dem Betrachter entgegen recken. Die weisse Glasur auf den Stielen ist absichtlich inkonsistent aufgebracht, wodurch ein uneinheitliches Weiss mit stellenweise schäumender Lavaglasur und Rissbildung erreicht wird. Die Münder der Stiele sind schmutzig violett-blau glasiert. Die Vorderseite des Spiegels ist eine schwarze Glasscheibe, die auf der Rückseite mit lichtabsorbierender Farbe bemalt wurde, um Ähnlichkeit mit dem ausgeschalteten Bildschirm eines Smartphones zu erzeugen.

«Schau in den Spiegel, was siehst Du dann? Ein Gesicht und ein Körper, die als unvollkommen gelten und all die Qual, die dabei mitschwingt.»

Building the work

This piece takes the form of an ornate mirror frame, Baroque or Rococo in inspiration, and is influenced by Paddy's interest in Ancient Greek mythology and medicine.

"I wanted to make something that looked fascinatingly horrible," says Paddy. The ornamentation for the mirror-frame is inspired by a fusion of the Gorgon Medusa, a winged creature with living snakes in place of hair, and a pedicle skin graft — a grafting technique whereby a piece of skin from a nearby area of the body remains attached at one of its corners, while the main part of the piece is reattached over the area that needs to be covered.

The Gorgon's snake-like hair is expressed in stubby, leech-like forms with wrinkles and seams and angry little mouths that reach out to the viewer. The white glaze on the pedicles is applied with conscious lack of consistency, creating an uneven white with foaming lava glaze in spots and uneven crazing. The mouths of the pedicles are of a dirty purplish-blue. The face of the mirror is a sheet of black glass whose reverse is painted with light-absorbing black paint to resemble... the blank screen of a switched-off smartphone.

"Look in the mirror, and what do you see? A face and body that are judged inadequate, and all the pain that goes with that."

HypoTrypanoPharmAlethephobia or: The Frustration of the Virologist

Die Konzeption des Werks

Diese Arbeit erkundet den enormen Erfolg von Impfstoff-Entwicklungsprogrammen und die darauf folgende Abneigung einiger Gemeinschaften und Personen, sich angesichts potentiell lebensbedrohlicher Krankheiten präventiv behandeln zu lassen. Es ist unbestreitbar, dass Impfstoffe für die Menschheit immens segensreich waren. Die Reaktion auf die COVID-19 Pandemie hat dies schlagend aufgezeigt und die Geschwindigkeit, in der die neuen Vakzine gegen COVID-19 entwickelt wurden, ist bemerkenswert. Jede pharmazeutische Intervention kann jedoch bei einigen Patienten unerwünschte Nebenwirkungen auslösen. Daran hat Paddy Hartley gedacht, als er seine Ideen für diese Arbeit entwickelte — ein Werk, das autobiographisch inspiriert ist, da ihn seine Mutter als Kind von Impfprogrammen abgemeldet hatte. «Ich wollte etwas herstellen, was meine Interessen und Ängste in diesem Alter darstellt», erinnert sich Paddy, «und dies mit einem Bezug zu den Falschinformationen, die heute über Impfstoffe verbreitet werden, versehen».

Der erste Teil des Titels, HypoTrypanoPharmAlethephobia, ist eine Synthese der Bezeichnungen von vier Phobien: Hypochondriasis (Angst vor Krankheit), Trypanophobie (Angst vor Nadeln und Injektionen), Pharmacophobie (Angst vor der Einnahme von Medikamenten) und Alethephobie (Angst vor der Wahrheit).

Der zweite Teil bezieht sich auf die Frustration, welche die Entwickler von Impfstoffen verspüren müssen, wenn Menschen sich dagegen zur Wehr setzen, sich gegen Krankheitsbilder impfen zu lassen, die eine massgebliche Bedrohung der öffentlichen Gesundheit darstellen. Die Form der Hydra ist aufgrund der traditionellen sowohl negativen wie positiven Assoziation der Schlange mit der Medizin gewählt. Ihr Gift kann als Antidot für gewisse Beschwerden verwendet werden; sie häuten sich, um eine neue Lebensphase zu beginnen; und sie sind in der jüngeren Vergangenheit mit medizinischer Quacksalberei in Verbindung gebracht worden, was im Begriff «snake-oil», welches von zynischen Opportunisten während des Kalifornischen Goldrauschs vertrieben wurde, widerhallt.

MEDIUM: Keramik, Nadeln
MASSE: 37–65 cm mit Podest, 4 Objekte
JAHR: 2021

HypoTrypanoPharmAlethephobia or: The Frustration of the Virologist

Imagining the work

This piece explores the huge success of vaccine development programmes and the subsequent reluctance of some communities and individuals to receive preventative treatment in the face of potentially life-threatening illnesses. There can be no question that vaccines have been enormously beneficial to humankind. The response to the COVID-19 pandemic has illustrated this perfectly, and the speed at which the new COVID-19 vaccines were developed is truly remarkable. Any pharmaceutical intervention has the potential, however, to cause unwanted side-effects in some patients. This was much on Paddy Hartley's mind as he developed his ideas for this work — a piece that is autobiographical in inspiration in that his mother opted him out of vaccination programmes when a child. "I wanted to make something that represented my interests and fears at that age," Paddy recollects, "and to combine this with reference to the misinformation peddled about vaccines today."

The first part of the title of the piece, *HypoTrypanoPharmAlethephobia*, is a synthesis of the names for four phobias: hypochondriasis (fear of illness), trypanophobia (fear of needles and injections), pharmacophobia (fear of taking medication), and alethephobia (fear of the truth).

The second part refers to the frustration that the developers of vaccines must feel when people refuse to be vaccinated against conditions that represent a major public health threat. The choice of a Hydra form draws on the traditional association, both positive and negative, of snakes with medicine. Their venom can be used as an antidote to certain medical conditions; they shed their skin to embark on a new phase of their existence; and they have been more recently associated with fraudulent medical claims in the form of the 'snake oil' widely peddled by cynical opportunists in America in the wake of the Californian Gold Rush.

MEDIA: Ceramic, needles
DIMENSIONS: 37–65 cm with stand, 4 objects

DATE: 2021

Herstellungsprozess

Das Erscheinungsbild der Hydra ist von den pulmonalen Arterien inspiriert, welche in die Lunge abzweigen, aber mit Injektionsnadeln anstelle von Zungen versehen sind. Die Giftzähne einer Schlange sind hohl und funktionieren wie eine Injektionsnadel, durch die das Gift von den Drüsen des Tiers in die Beute gelangt. Paddy wollte hingegen die Zunge selbst durch eine Nadel darstellen, um anzudeuten, dass diese keinen Schaden verursachen soll.

Als Aufbaumethode kam eine Mischung verschiedener Modelliertechniken zum Einsatz, darunter das Ziehen von Tonkringeln oder auch hohler Tonröhren, ganz wie wenn man am Henkel einer Tasse ziehen würde. Die Äste der Hydra wurden aus Porzellanpapier hergestellt und zunächst getrocknet, bevor sie in ledrig ausgehärtetem Zustand am Körper befestigt wurden, der aus demselben Material besteht.

Dieses Werk zu brennen war ausserordentlich schwierig, da Porzellanpapier im Brand um rund 20 Prozent schrumpft und die oberen Äste der Struktur während der drei unterschiedlichen Brände gestützt werden mussten. Die Hydra wurde danach mit einer Steinzeugglasur bei einer deutlich tieferen Temperatur gebrannt. Die Steinzeugglasur bildet *craquelé* und ist transparent, aber der Körper der Hydra ist mit Flecken einer weinroten Glasur übersät, welche Kristalle ausbildet, die an Einstichwunden erinnern. «Die Hydra ist eine sich selbst verletzende, selbstimpfende Kreatur», reflektiert Paddy.

«Die Hydra ist eine selbst-verletzende, sich selbst-impfende Kreatur.»

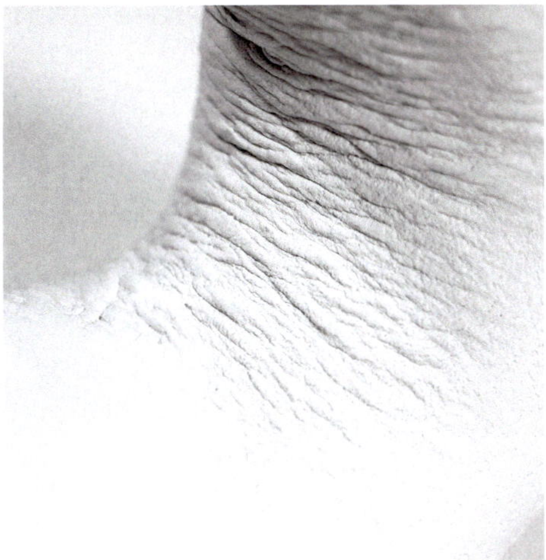

Building the work

The form of the Hydra is inspired by the pulmonary arteries that branch into the lungs, but with hypodermic needles for tongues. The fang of a snake is hollow and acts like a hypodermic needle, pumping venom from the animal's glands into the prey. Paddy, however, wanted the tongue itself to the represented by a needle, implying that the needle was not designed to do harm. The build method was an amalgamation of modelling techniques, and involved pulling at solid loops of clay or hollow extruded tubes as one would pull on the handle of a mug or teacup. The Hydra's branches were made from porcelain paper clay and left to go leather-hard before being attached to the body, which is of the same material.

Firing this work was exceptionally challenging, since porcelain paper clay shrinks by up to 20 per cent when fired and the upper projections of the branching structure required support during a process involving three separate firings. The Hydra was then glazed with an earthenware glaze and fired at a much lower temperature. This earthenware glaze is crazed and transparent, but the body of the Hydra is peppered with touches of maroon glaze crystals suggestive of puncture wounds. "The Hydra is a self-harming, self-inoculating creature," reflects Paddy.

"The Hydra is a self-harming, self-inoculating creature."

The Infinity Balance

Die Konzeption des Werks

Diese Arbeit ermutigt, über die sozialen Konsequenzen von Pharmazeutika nachzudenken. Im Besonderen lädt sie dazu ein, die breite Verwendung von oralen Kontrazeptiva und deren Einfluss auf das Durchschnittsalter der globalen Bevölkerung zu rezipieren — auffällig ist hierbei die wachsende Altersdifferenz zwischen den Älteren und den Jüngeren in westlichen Gesellschaften. Parallel zu den Verbesserungen im Gesundheitswesen, der Hygiene und der Ernährung, die zu einer erhöhten Lebenserwartung geführt haben, hat die Einführung der Kontrazeptiva zu der wachsenden Altersdifferenz beigetragen. Diese Faktoren haben ihrerseits zum Anstieg altersbedingter Erkrankungen beigetragen, was zu Befürchtungen bezüglich des Pflegeaufwands geführt hat — ein Trend, der künftig eine soziale Krise auslösen könnte.

Während des «Challenge of Life» Symposiums 1971 war eines der grossen Anliegen die damals vorhergesagte «Bevölkerungsexplosion». Diese Ängste haben sich nie bewahrheitet. Obwohl die Weltbevölkerung im vergangenen halben Jahrhundert stark zugenommen hat, wuchs sie nie in dem befürchteten Ausmass an und die aktuelle globale Zahl an Menschen hat vor kurzem sogar begonnen, abzunehmen.

«Die Infinity Balance anerkennt, dass besonders die Kontrazeptiva die Altersstruktur der Weltbevölkerung verändert haben, aufgrund fallender Geburtenzahlen und Menschen, die sich erst später im Leben für Kinder entscheiden,» erklärt Paddy. Während dies zum Gegenteil der befürchteten Bevölkerungsexplosion führt, hat dieser Trend dennoch negative Folgen. Der Anstieg des Anteils der Älteren schafft neue Schwierigkeiten: Pensionskassen stehen unter Druck, da die Lebenserwartung zunimmt und im Pflegesektor verlangt der Anstieg altersbedingter Krankheiten nach einem höheren Einsatz. Bezüglich sowohl finanzieller als auch nicht-finanzieller Ressourcen stellt dieser demographische Wandel ein Problem dar, dem sich die Welt erst stellen muss. Die befürchtete Bevölkerungsexplosion ist durch ein völlig anders geartetes Problem ersetzt worden. «Die Botschaft dieses Werks ist optimistisch,» überlegt Paddy. «Sie legt einen unendlich verstellbaren Ausgleichsprozess nahe, durch den unvorhergesehene Faktoren die sorgfältigst erarbeiteten pessimistischen Prognosen über den Haufen werfen.»

MEDIUM: Stahl, Glas, Porzellan, Ketten, Sand
MASSE: 190 × 68 × 22 cm

JAHR: 2021

The Infinity Balance

Imagining the work

This piece encourages reflection on the far-reaching societal consequences of pharmaceuticals and how these are prescribed. In particular, it invites consideration of the widespread application of the contraceptive pill and its influence on the average age of the global population, most noticeably in the form of the growing age gap between the old and the young in western societies. In parallel with improvements in healthcare, sanitation and diet, which have led to an increase in life expectancy, the implementation of the contraceptive pill has contributed significantly to a widening of the age gap. These factors have in turn fuelled the growth of age-related diseases, triggering concerns regarding the burden these are perceived to be placing on the caring professions – a trend which may well hold the seeds of a future societal crisis.

At the 'Challenge of Life' Symposium in 1971, great concern was expressed in the face of a predicted 'population explosion'. These fears were never realised. Although the world's population has increased significantly in the past half-century, growth has not occurred on the scale imagined, and the current global total has in fact recently started to decline.

"The Infinity Balance acknowledges how the advent of the contraceptive pill in particular has changed the age structure of the world's population, with birth rates falling and people opting to have children later in life," explains Paddy. While the reverse of the feared population explosion, this trend nevertheless has negative consequences. The rise in the proportion of elderly people in society is creating a new challenge: it places more and more pressure on pension funds because people are living longer, and on the caregiving sector because it is associated with an overall increase in age-related diseases that require management. In terms of both financial and non-financial resources, this demographic shift is a problem that the world has yet to fully address. The feared population explosion has been replaced by a completely different problem. "The message of this artwork in an optimistic one," muses Paddy. "It shows an infinitely adjustable balancing process whereby unforeseen factors upset even the most meticulously researched pessimistic predictions."

MEDIA: Steel, glass, porcelain, chains, sand
DIMENSIONS: 190 × 68 × 22 cm

DATE: 2021

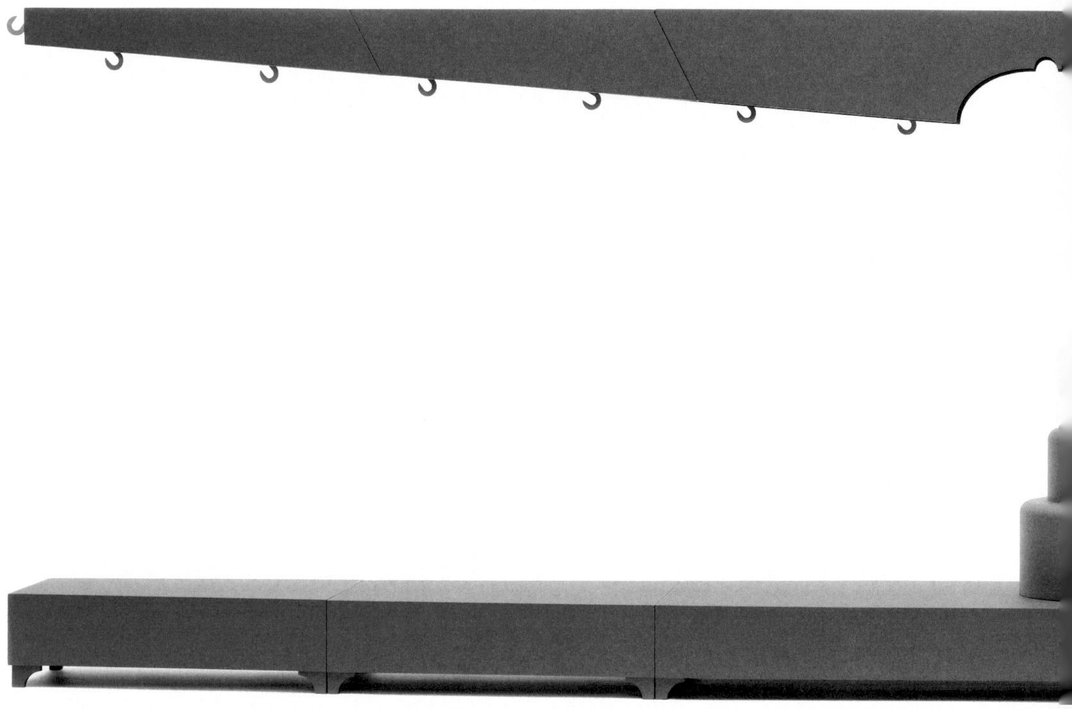

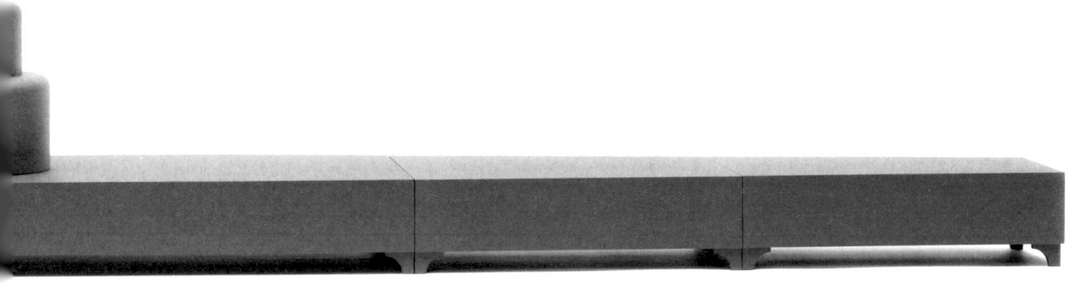

«Die Botschaft dieses Werks ist optimistisch. Sie legt einen unendlich verstellbaren Ausgleichsprozess nahe.»

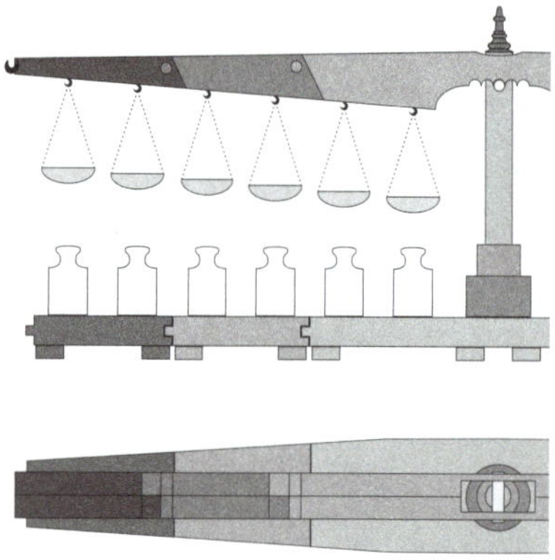

Herstellungsprozess

The Infinity Balance nimmt die Form einer unendlich verstellbaren, modularen, stilisierten Apothekenwaage an. Jedes Element der Waage ist verstellbar, um Ausgleich zu erzielen. Der modulare Wiegebalken, der beinahe zwei Meter misst, kann nach Bedarf mit zusätzlichen Elementen verlängert oder verkürzt werden. Der Achsenpunkt am Arm kann nach links oder rechts verschoben werden. Auch ist es möglich, die 12 abgehängten Schalen zu entfernen und mit tieferen Gefässen zu ersetzen. Häkchen an beiden Enden der Waage können andere Schalen aufnehmen, um zur Erhaltung der Balance beizutragen. Die Basis kann verlängert oder verkürzt werden.

Die hohlen, mundgeblasenen Gefässe in Form von Gewichten unter jeder Schale enthalten Sand, was ermöglicht, das Gewicht zu verändern. Die Einteilungen auf den Glasgewichten repräsentieren die Altersgruppen 0–10 Jahre, 10–20, 20–30 und so weiter, bis 120. Diese Einteilungen laufen beidseitig von 0–10 und 10–0. Der Sand in den Glasgewichten beginnt im 0–10-Gewicht in rein weiss und wird dann immer dunkler, bis er im 110–120-Gewicht ganz schwarz ist. Die Waage selbst ist grau: Weder Schwarz noch weiss, sondern irgendwo in der Mitte.

The Infinity Balance wurde unter Einbezug verschiedener Fachleute konstruiert. Paddys erstes Konzept und sein Design wurden durch Chris Radtke in technische Details und eine geeignete Mechanik umgesetzt, die Waage selbst wurde dann bei Grünthal Feinblechtechnik gefertigt. Die Gewichte wurden nach Paddys Design durch die Glasbläser von Roche Basel hergestellt. Paddy selbst hat die Keramikschalen gefertigt, die am Wiegebalken hängen. «Von Beginn dieser Zusammenarbeit an wollte ich Menschen von Roche in den Bauprozess involvieren,» sagt Paddy. «Ich bin hocherfreut, dass sie bei der Realisierung des fertigen Kunstwerks eine Rolle gespielt haben.»

Building the work

The Infinity Balance takes the form of a set of infinitely adjustable, modular, stylised apothecary scales. Every element of the scales can be adjusted to achieve balance. The modular balance arm, almost two metres in span, can be lengthened or shortened with additional components should these be required. The central balance pivot point on the arm can be shifted to the left or right. The 12 suspended dishes can be removed and replaced by deeper receptacles. Hooks at either end of the scale can accommodate another dish to help maintain the balance. The base can be expanded or reduced in size.

The hollow blown-glaze weights under each dish contain sand, allowing the mass of the weight to be changed. The divisions on the glass weights represent the age groups 0–10 years, 10–20, 20–30 and so on, up to 120, and these divisions are represented running from 0–10 and from 10–0. The sand in the glass weights begins pure white in the 0–10 weight, becoming progressively darker until in the 110–120 weight it is black. The scales themselves are grey: neither black nor white, they are somewhere in the middle.

The Infinity Balance is a collaborative artwork in its construction. From Paddy's initial concept and design, the technical detailing of the mechanics of the form were realised by Chris Radtke and constructed by Grünthal Feinblechtechnik. The weights were created to Paddy's design by Roche's own glass craftsmen. Paddy himself made the ceramic dishes that are suspended from the balance arm. "From the outset of this collaboration, I wanted to have people from Roche involved in the build," says Paddy. "I'm delighted they played a part in the realisation of the finished piece."

"The message of this artwork is one of optimism. It suggests an infinitely adjustable balancing process."

Retro—spective

Auswahl der Werke
1999–2021

Artworks
1999–2021

Splint

Die Konzeption des Werks

Diese Arbeiten sind inspiriert von Menschen, welche Heilung durch die Kraft des Gebets befürworten. Hüftgelenk-Implantate wirken als inneres Hilfsmittel, wie eine orthopädische Schiene (splint), die den Heilungsprozess unterstützt. So wird ein direkter Kontrast zum Kreuz erzeugt, das ein äusserliches «Hilfsmittel» darstellte, den Tod des daran aufgehängten Individuums herbeizuführen.

Splint I
MEDIUM: Hüftgelenk-Implantate
MASSE: 60 × 38 × 9 cm

Splint II
MEDIUM: Hüftgelenk-Implantate
MASSE: 60 × 40 × 6 cm

Splint III
MEDIUM: Hüftgelenk-Implantate
MASSE: 44 × 30 × 5 cm

JAHR: 1999/2000

Teil der Installation «Safe from Harm»*

* Splint, Rosary and Crown of Thorns entstammen der «Safe from Harm» Installation und wurden als Reaktion auf Gespäche mit Menschen geschaffen, die unterschiedliche religiöse Gruppen repräsentieren und welche zu ihrer Beziehung zur Medizin und zu medizinischen Eingriffen und Technologien befragt wurden. Die Werke kritisieren nicht ein spezifisches Glaubenssystem. Vielmehr wurden die Titel aus den Haltungen und Ideen inspiriert, die aus den Diskussionen entstanden sind, welche die Gegensätze in diesen Glaubensbekenntnissen und die sich verschiebenden Haltungen anerkennen und dem Denkprozess der Befragten entsprechen.

Splint

Imagining the work

Inspired by individuals who are advocating the power of prayer to heal. Hip replacement implants act as internal splints involved in the healing process. A direct contrast to the Cross, which is an external splint used to bring about the death of the individual it supports.

Splint I
MEDIA: Hip replacement components
DIMENSIONS: 60 × 38 × 9 cm

Splint II
MEDIA: Hip replacement components
DIMENSIONS: 60 × 40 × 6 cm

Splint III
MEDIA: Hip replacement components
DIMENSIONS: 44 × 30 × 5 cm

DATE: 1999/2000

Part of the 'Safe from Harm' artwork*

* Splint, Rosary and Crown of Thorns form the 'Safe from Harm' artwork and were created in response to conversations with people representing various religious groups about their relationships with medicine and medical interventions and technology. The works are not a critique of specific belief systems. Rather, the attitudes and ideas that emerged from these discussions inspired these words, which recognise contradictions in these beliefs and shifting attitudes that suit the thought process of those with these conversations were conducted.

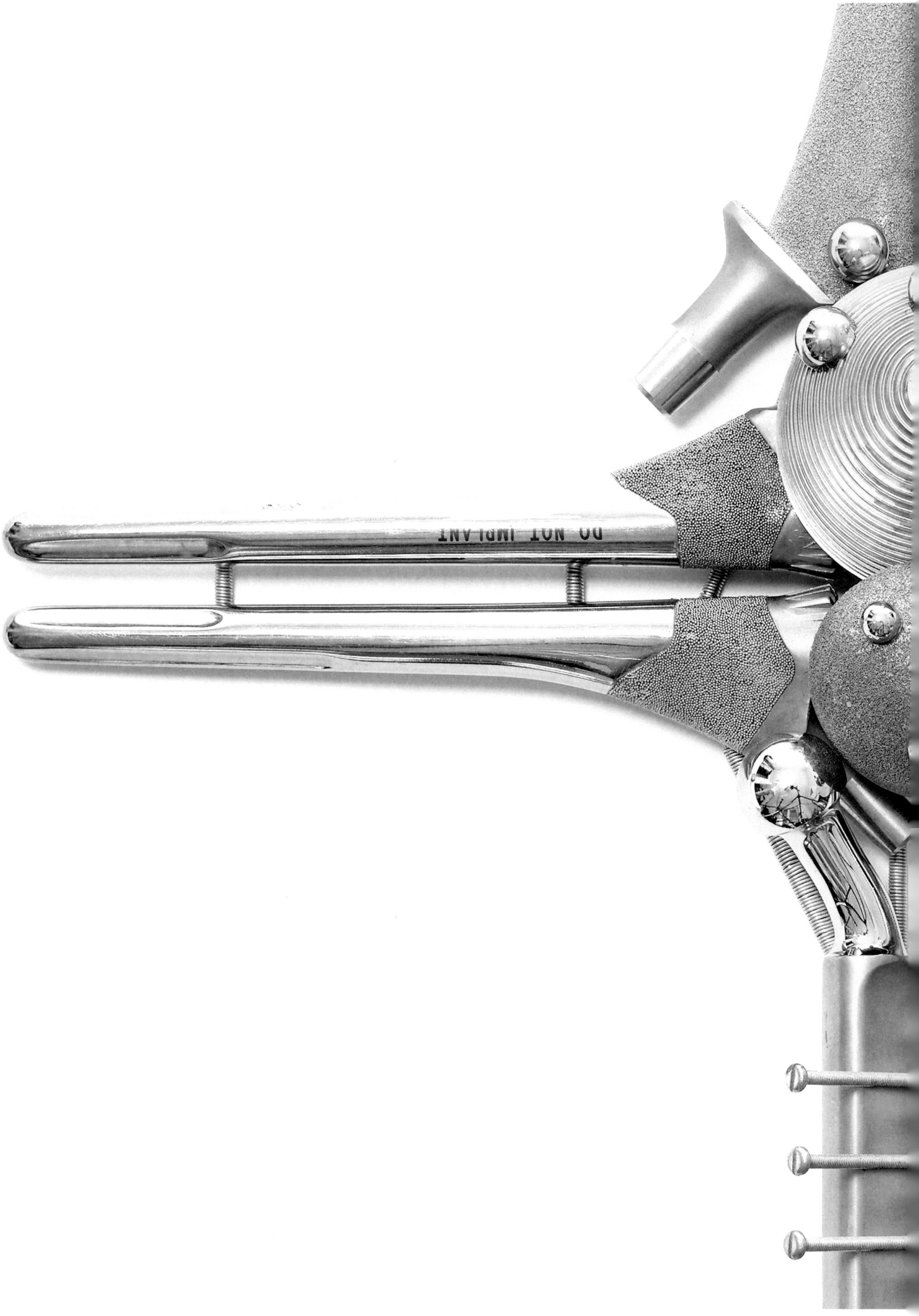
DO NOT IMPLANT

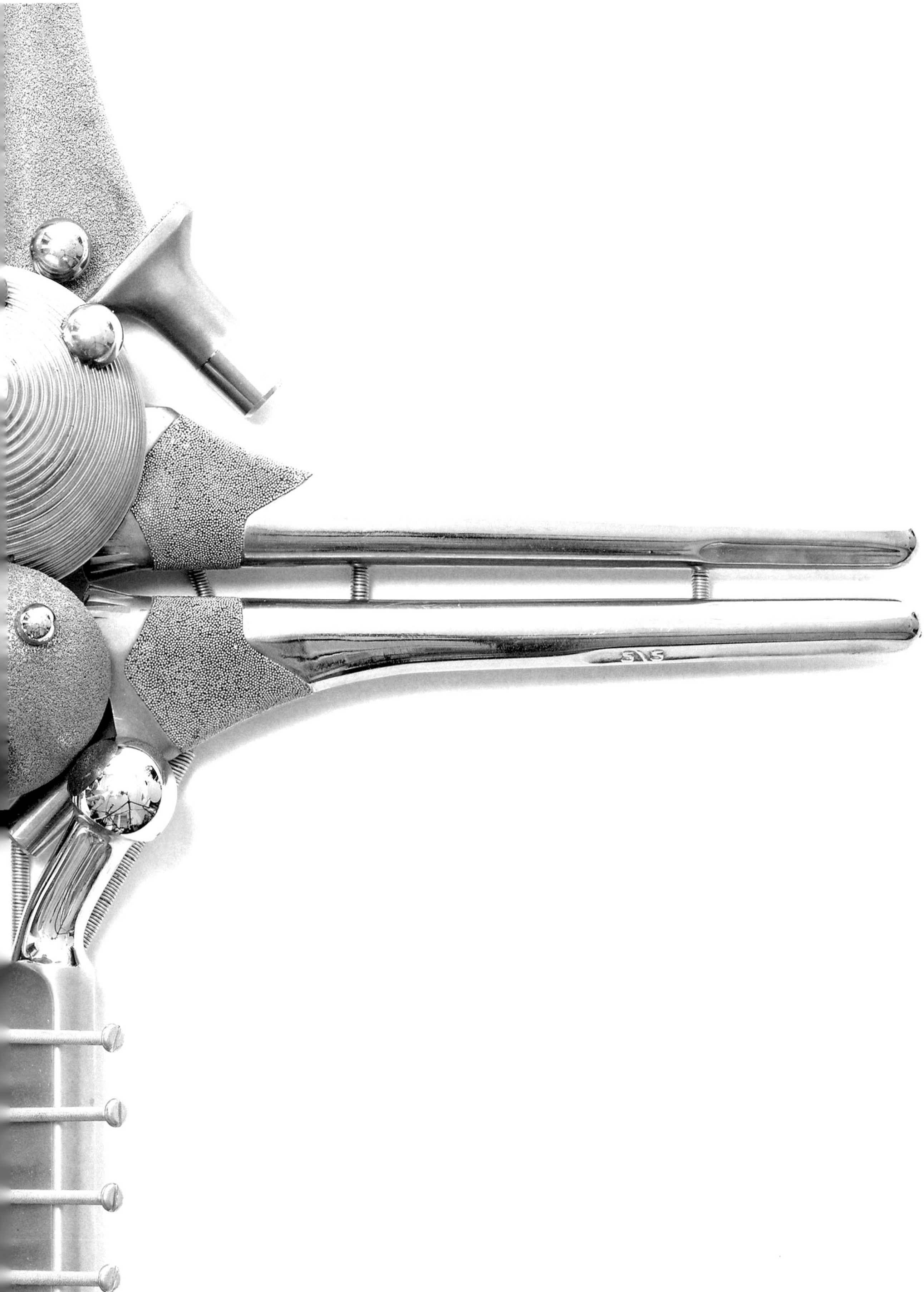

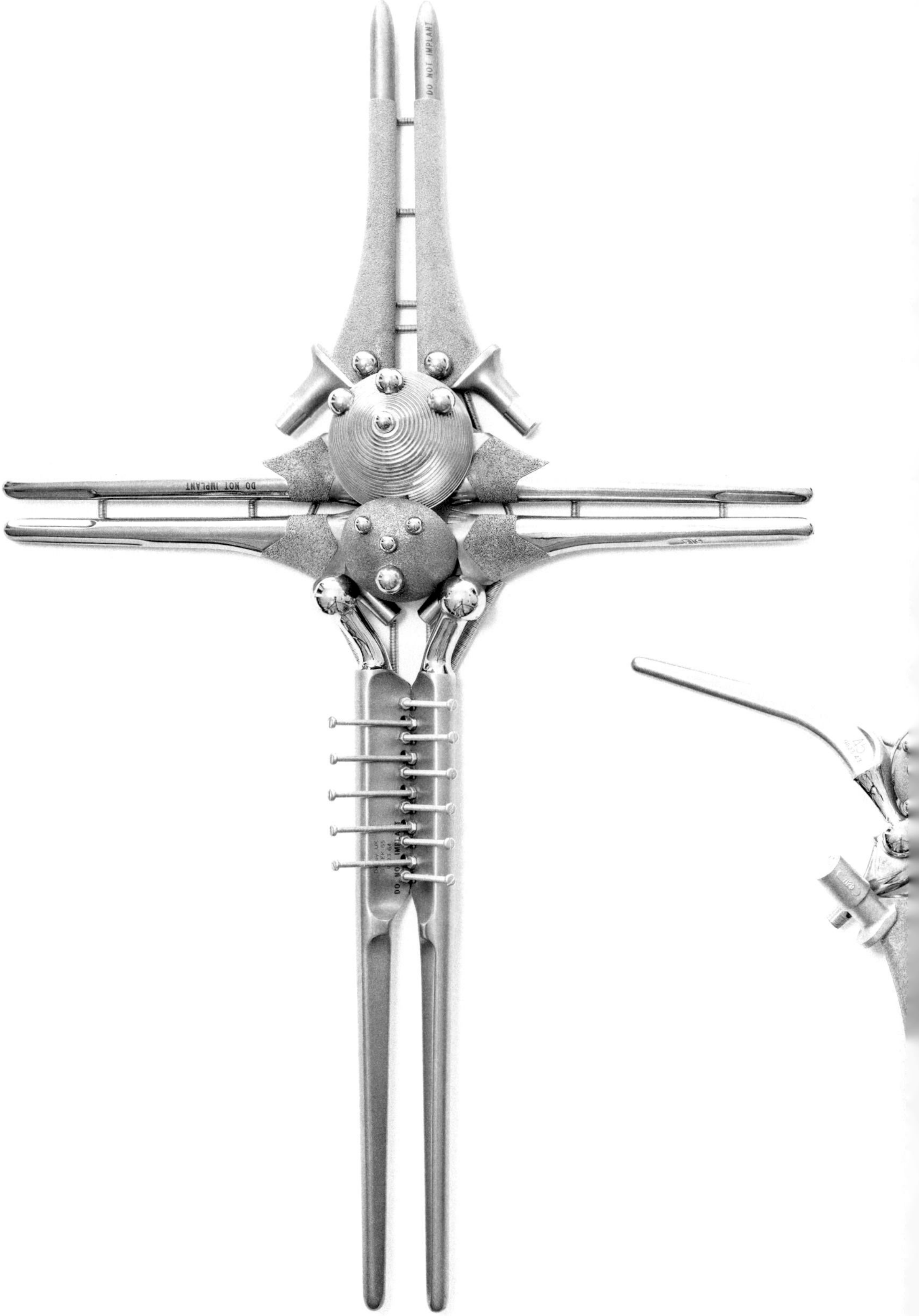

Splint II, Splint III, Splint I

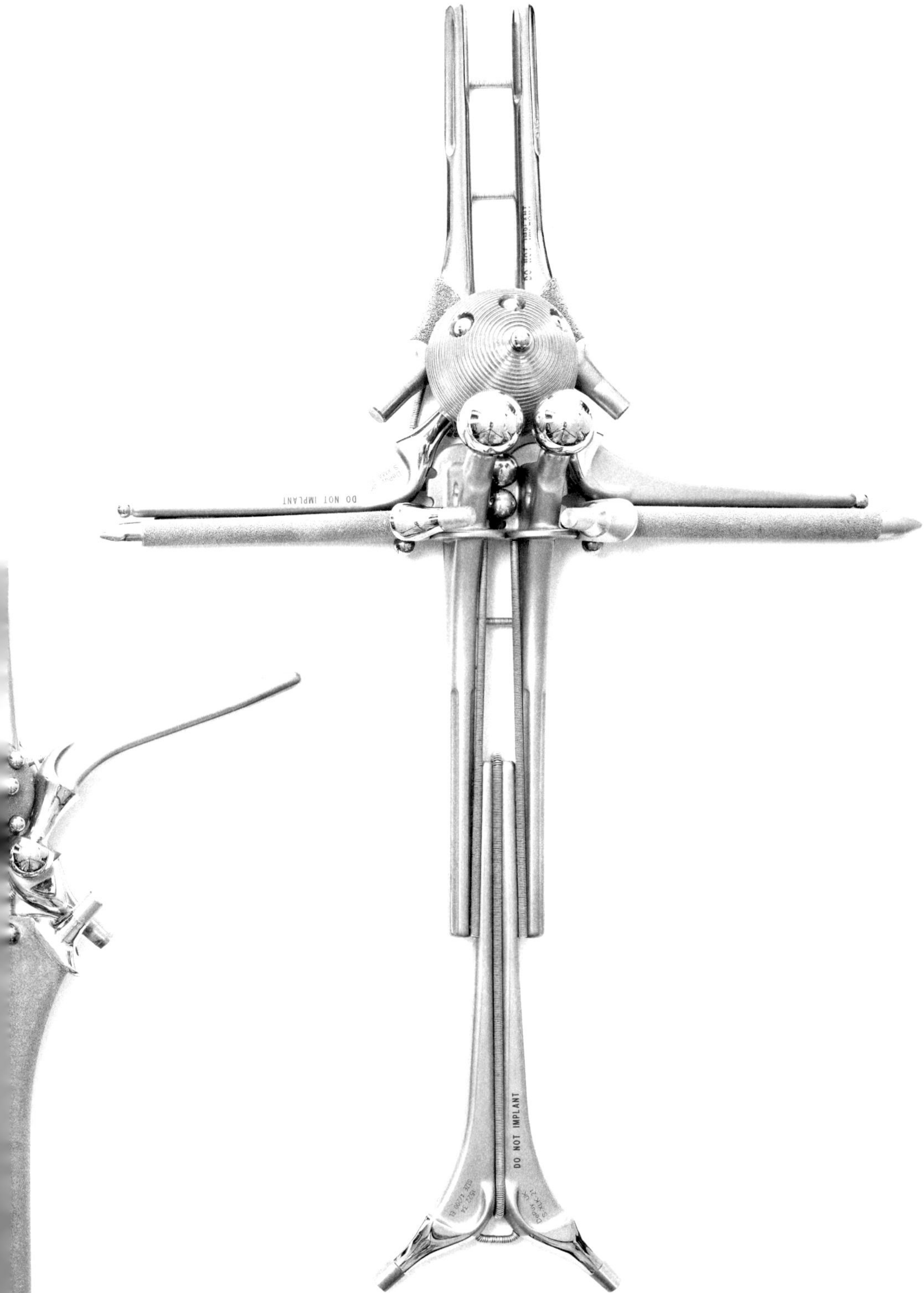
DO NOT IMPLANT
DO NOT IMPLANT

Rosary

Die Konzeption des Werks

Diese Arbeit stellt einen Kommentar zu der Abhängigkeit von Medikamenten und religiösem Glauben dar. Beide können als nützlich, abhängig machend, abträglich und potentiell dem Missbrauch ausgesetzt angesehen werden, sowohl durch die Nutzer wie auch derer, die darauf basierende Ideen verbreiten. Rosary II wurde über 20 Jahre nach den ursprünglichen Rosary-Werken geschaffen. Diese erneuerte Version beinhaltet Pharmazeutika, die als Prozac und Viagra verkauft wurden, deren Beschaffung online im Internet erschreckend einfach war.

Rosary I
MEDIUM: Prozac, Viagra, Kanülen, chirurgischer Nähfaden, Teile eines Stethoskops
MASSE: Maximale Länge 65 cm

JAHR: 1999/2000

Rosary II
MEDIUM: Medikamente, die online als Prozac oder Viagra verkauft wurden, Kanülen, chirurgischer Nähfaden, Präparierhaken, Bumerangnadeln
MASSE: Maximale Länge 65 cm

JAHR: 2021

Teil der Installation «Safe from Harm»*
(Siehe auch Seite 120)

Rosary

Imagining the work

A commentary on the nature of addiction and dependence on pharmaceuticals and religious belief. Both can be considered beneficial, addictive, detrimental and subject to abuse by the user and also by those supplying/promoting ideas based on these elements. The new Rosary II piece was created more than 20 years since the creation of the original Rosary artwork — an updated version featuring pharmaceuticals sold as Prozac and Viagra, which were found to be alarmingly easy to source online.

Rosary I
MEDIA: Prozac, Viagra, cannula, suture thread, stethoscope component
DIMENSIONS: Maximum length 65 cm

DATE: 1999/2000

Rosary II
MEDIA: Pharmaceuticals sold online as Prozac and Viagra, cannula, suture thread, dissecting hooks, boomerang needles
DIMENSIONS: Maximum length 65 cm

DATE: 2021

Part of the 'Safe from Harm' artwork* (please refer to the page 121)

Rosary I, Rosary II

Crown of Thorns

Die Konzeption des Werks

Als Antwort zu den sich verschiebenden Haltungen religiöser Gruppen gegenüber der biomedizinischen Forschung und der Anwendung medizinischer Technologien — spezifisch der Klontechnologien — geschaffen. Die «Crown of Thorns» besteht aus einer post-mortem Schädelzwinge, die mit dem Lebensende assoziiert ist und Glaspipetten. Die Pipette ist in diesem Fall eine Referenz an das künstlich kreierte Leben und wird gemeinhin mit medizinischer Forschung und Anwendung, auch der In-Vitro-Fertilisation (IVF), in Verbindung gebracht. Das Werk ähnelt absichtlich einem Heiligenschein sowie der Dornenkrone, die in der christlichen Bildikonographie allgegenwärtig ist und den Beginn sowie das Ende des Lebens darstellt.

MEDIUM: Schädelzwinge, Glaspipetten, Spiegel
MASSE: Spiegeldurchmesser: 80 cm. Höhe der zentralen Glaspipetten: ca. 35 cm

JAHR: 1999/2000

Teil der Installation «Safe from Harm»*
(Siehe auch Seite 120)

Crown of Thorns

Imagining the work

Created in response to the shifting attitudes expressed by religious groups regarding biomedical research and the application of medical technologies — specifically, cloning technologies. The Crown of Thorns is formed from a post-mortem skull coronet, associated with the end of life, and glass Pasteur pipettes. The pipette in this instance references the beginning of artificially created life and is an object commonly associated with medical research and applications, including in vitro fertilisation (IVF). The piece intentionally resembles the halo and the Crown of Thorns depicted in much Christian imagery, and represents the beginning and the end of life.

MEDIA: Skull coronet, Pasteur pipettes, mirror
DIMENSIONS: Mirror diameter: 80 cm; central glass pipette height: c. 35 cm

DATE: 1999/2000

Part of the 'Safe from Harm' artwork*
(please refer to the page 121)

OnLine

Die Konzeption des Werks

Als Konsequenz der Onlinerecherche und Beschaffung von Prozac und Viagra in der Frühzeit des Internets, stellen diese Stücke einen kreativen Exkurs dar, der sich aus der Herstellung der Arbeit «Rosary» ergeben hat. Sie wurden durch die Erkenntnis inspiriert, wie einfach es war (und immer noch ist), eine Selbstdiagnose zu stellen und sich selber Medikamente zu verschreiben, indem man das Internet als Recherche- und Marktressource nutzt. Diese unregulierte und unüberwachte Beschaffung kann missbraucht werden und führt zu einer breiten Vielfalt von Abhängigkeiten.

MEDIUM: Pharmazeutische Kapseln, Fischerhaken
MASSE: Variabel, ca. 5 × 5 cm

JAHR: 1999/2000

OnLine

Imagining the work

Created as a consequence of researching and sourcing Prozac and Viagra online in the early days of the Internet, these pieces were a creative digression that evolved from the making of 'Rosary'. They were inspired by the realisation of how easy it was (and still is) to self-diagnose and self-prescribe using the Internet as a research and purchasing resource. This unregulated and unmonitored sourcing can be abused and lead to a wide range of addictions.

MEDIA: Pharmaceutical capsules, fishing hooks
DIMENSIONS: c. 5 × 5 cm

DATE: 1999/2000

20 mg

PainKiller

Die Konzeption des Werks

Wenige Jahre nach Aufenthalten am Thackray Museum of Medicine und den Royal Armouries Leeds geschaffen, ist diese Arbeit von den Eindrücken inspiriert, die der Künstler anlässlich der Reaktionen der Öffentlichkeit auf Ausstellungen chirurgischer Instrumente und Waffen gewonnen hat. Dieses Werk ergründet die Dualität unserer Furcht vor medizinischen Gerätschaften und Eingriffen (erdacht, um den Heilungsprozess zu befördern) und unserer Faszination für Waffen (erdacht, um zu verletzen), die wir sowohl personalisieren wie auch als Fetisch betrachten.

MEDIUM: Artefakte aus dem Labormüll
MASSE: 18 × 38 × 5 cm

JAHR: 2013

PainKiller

Imagining the work

Created a few years after residencies conducted concurrently at the Thackray Museum of Medicine and the Royal Armouries, Leeds, and inspired by the artist's observations of the public reacting to exhibits of surgical instruments and weapons. This piece explores the duality of our fear of medical devices and medical interventions (conceived to facilitate the healing process) and our fascination with, personalisation of, and fetishization of weapons (conceived to do harm).

MEDIA: Laboratory salvage
DIMENSIONS: 18 × 38 × 5 cm

DATE: 2013

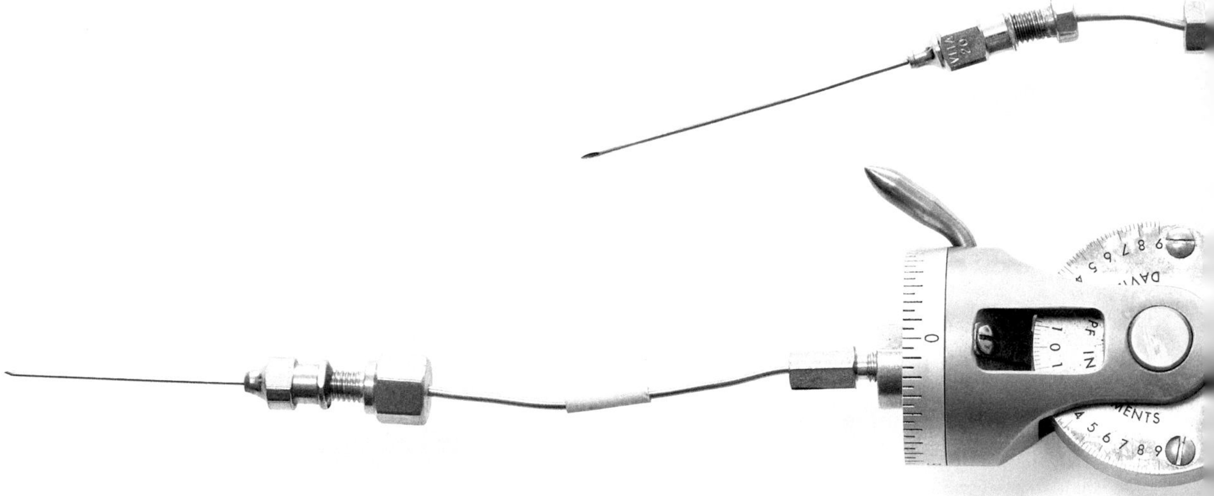

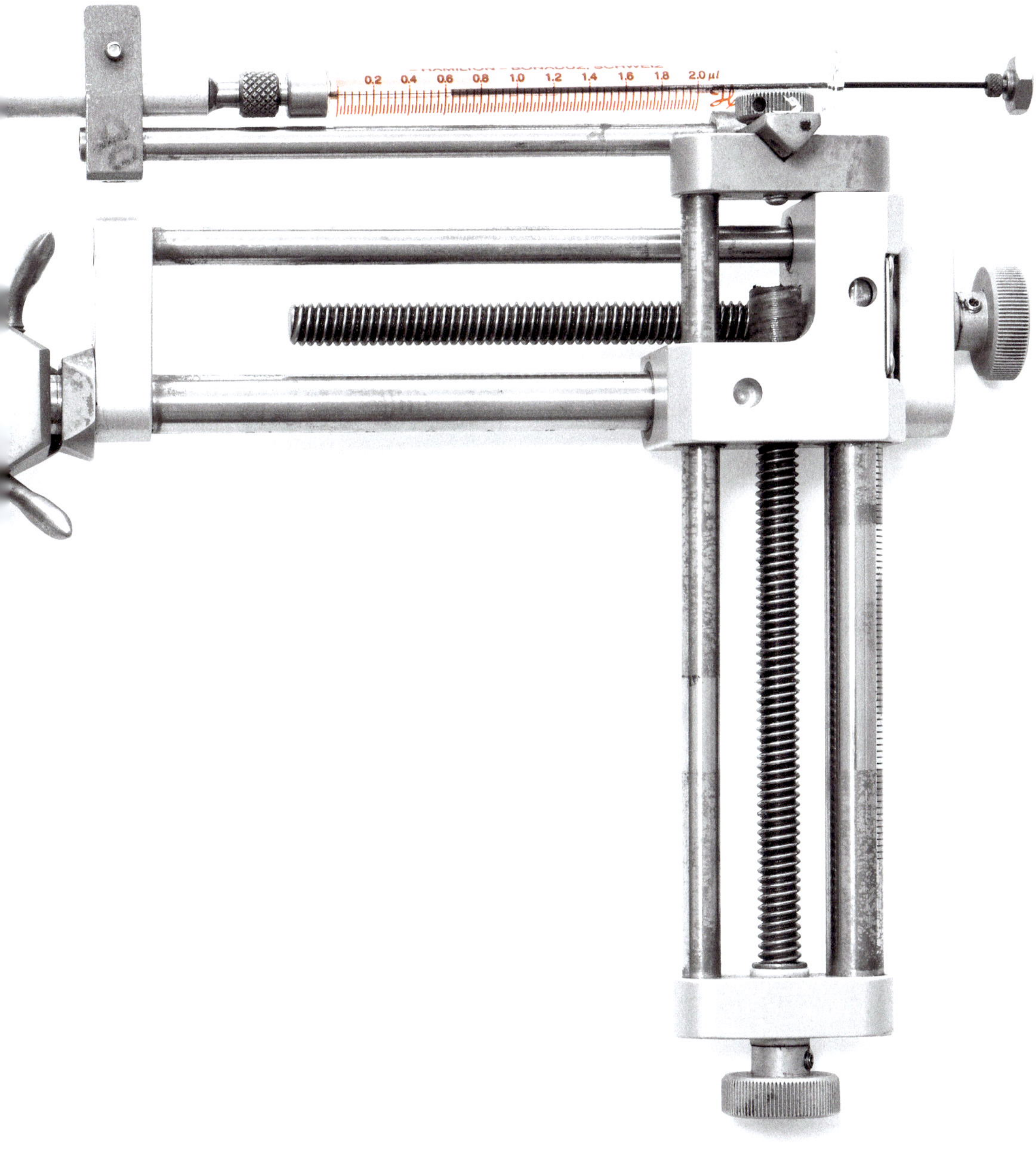
0.2 0.4 0.6 0.8 1.0 1.2 1.4 1.6 1.8 2.0 µl

The Aligera Series

Die Konzeption des Werks

Ein kreativer Exkurs kam während der Arbeit an der Papaver Rhoeas Mohnblumen-Installation zustande. Schnitte von Lammherz-Gewebe werden auf einem Leuchtkasten fotografiert und mit minimaler digitaler Manipulation behandelt, um den Eindruck von geflügelten Formen zu erzeugen, die durch Entomologie und Meeresbiologie inspiriert sind.

MEDIUM: Digitaler C-Typ Druck auf Fujiflex Papier, aufgezogen auf Aluminium mit Unterrahmen. Digitale Fotografie, die Komposition aus Lammherz-Gewebeschnitten
MASSE: Bis 100 × 100 cm

JAHR: 2015

The Aligera Series

Imagining the work

A creative digression that came about during the making of the Papaver Rhoeas poppy sculptures. Slices of lamb's-heart tissue are shot on a lightbox and minimal digital manipulation is applied to create a series of winged forms inspired by entomological and marine biology forms.

MEDIA: Digital C-type print on Fujiflex paper on aluminium with subframe mount; digital photography composition of lamb's-heart tissue slices
DIMENSIONS: Up to 100 × 100 cm

DATE: 2015

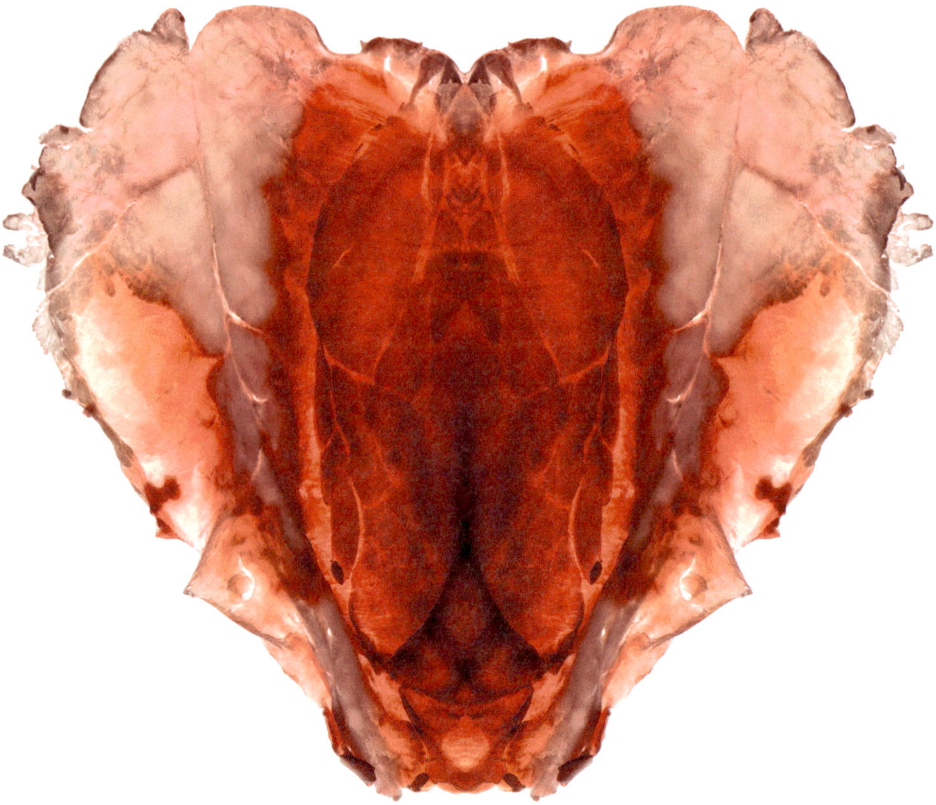

Cruor fructus ūnus (blood fruit)

 Myliobatoidei duo

Rhopalocera ūnus

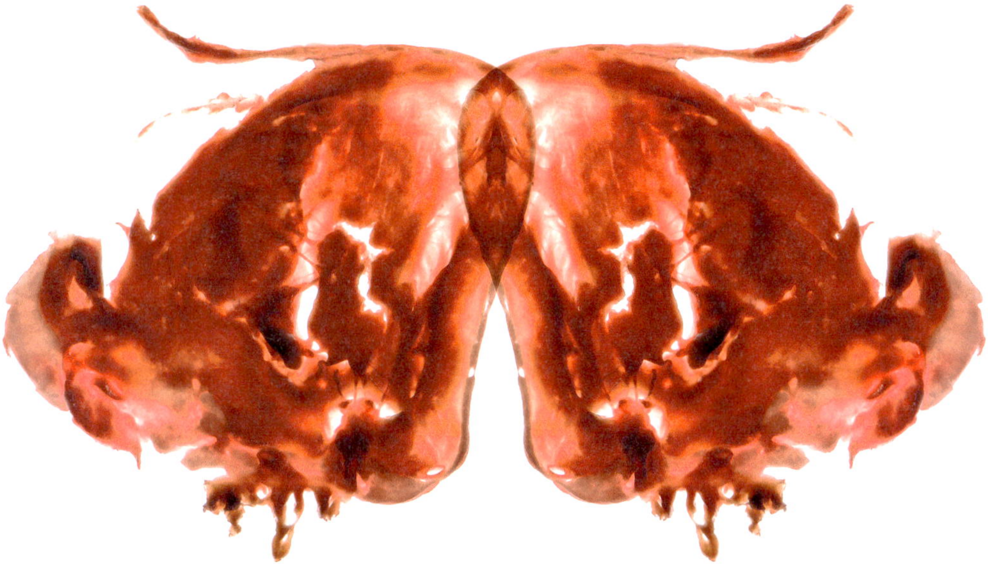

 Heterocera septum

Myliobatoidei quīnque

Consequence

Die Konzeption des Werks

Das Werk wurde als Erwiderung auf die Veränderung der Vorschriften zur Brandschutzkleidung an Bord von Schiffen im Ersten Weltkrieg und auch auf die rekonstruktive Chirurgie, die der Uhrmacher und Marinegefreite William Vicarage an seinen Händen durchführen liess, um diese wieder funktionsfähig zu machen, geschaffen.

MEDIUM: Porcelain
MASSE: 40 × 30 × 12 cm

JAHR: 2017

Consequence

Imagining the work

Created in response to the change in protocol regarding fire protection clothing to be worn aboard ship during World War I and also in response to the reconstructive surgery that watchmaker and Royal Navy Able Seaman William Vicarage underwent to restore function to his hands.

MEDIA: Porcelain
DIMENSIONS: 40 × 30 × 12 cm

DATE: 2017

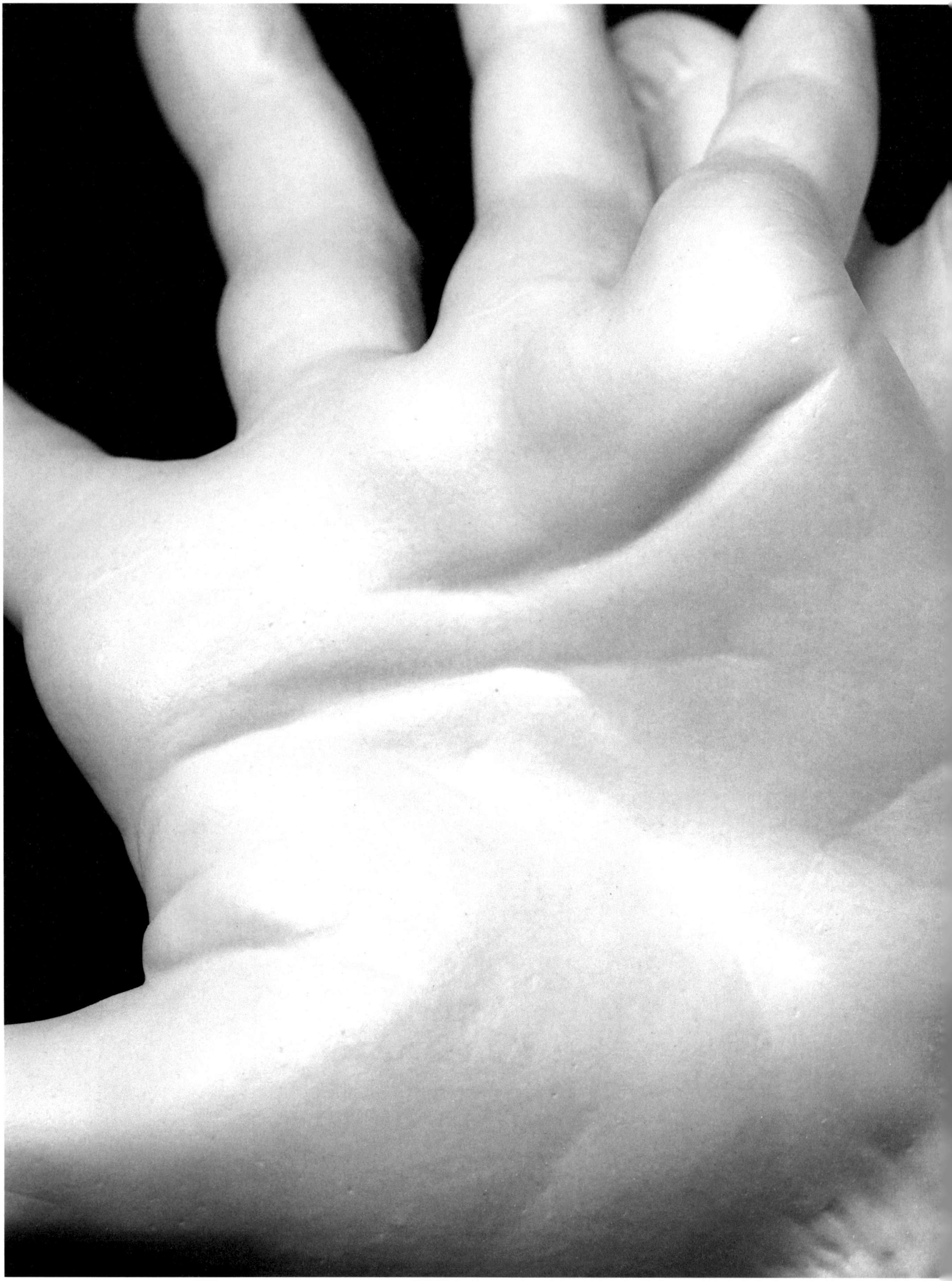

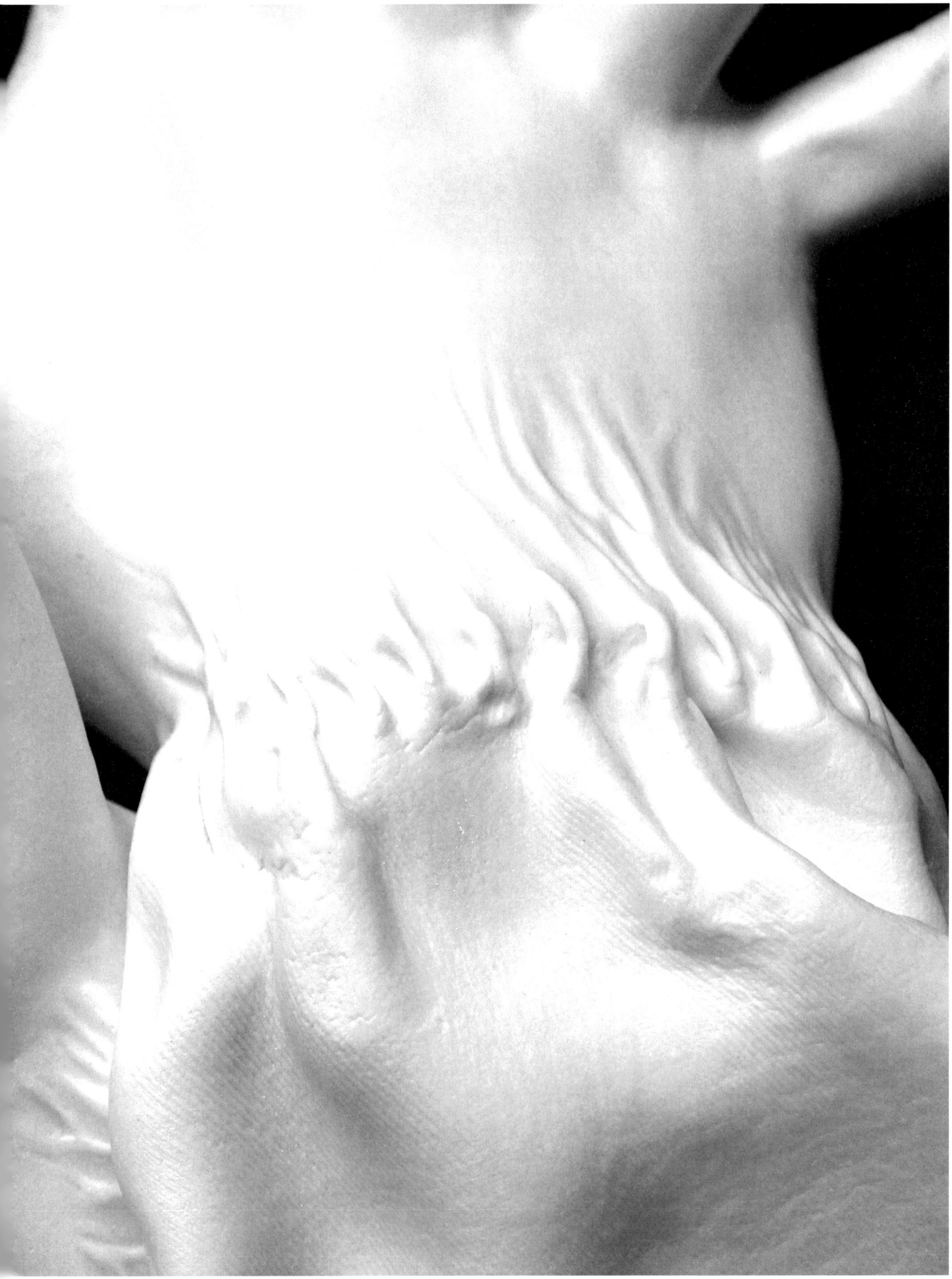

Make my move for me, will you, my Love

Die Konzeption des Werks

Diese Arbeit stellt den Höhepunkt von 15 Jahren Forschung an der Geschichte Britischer Veteranen dar, die im Ersten Weltkrieg Gesichtsverletzungen erlitten hatten, und sich rekonstruktiver Gesichtschirurgie durch den Pionier Sir Harold Gillies unterziehen liessen. Sie wurde durch die Geschichte des Marinegefreiten William Vicarage inspiriert, dem ersten Britischen Veteranen, dessen Gesicht mittels der Technik langgestielter Stranglappen rekonstruiert wurde sowie durch Paddy Hartleys spätere Gespräche mit seiner Enkelin. William leistete in der Royal Navy auf der HMS Malaya Dienst als Mitglied der 5. Schlachtstaffel unter Sir Hugh Evan-Thomas. Er erlitt während der Schlacht um Jütland (31. Mai – 1. Juni 1916) schwere Korditverbrennungen am Gesicht und an den Händen.

Bevor Paddy Hartley seine Familie kennenlernte, gab es keine öffentlichen Dokumente zu Williams Erfahrungen. Diese Lücke zu schliessen war ein Höhepunkt der beruflichen Karriere des Künstlers. Es bleibt zu hoffen, dass die Einsichten, die während des Projekts aufgedeckt wurden, die Anerkennung des enorm wichtigen Beitrags der Erfahrungen Williams in der Entwicklung der rekonstruktiven Gesichtschirurgie fördern werden. Mehr über William kann unter http://paddyhartley.com/vicarage-1 nachgelesen werden.

«Make my move for me, will you, my Love» kombiniert Referenzen zu Williams später Lebensgeschichte. Sein ursprüngliches Tätigkeitsgebiet als Uhrmacher zeigt sich in den Solitärzählern, das Spielbrett aus Porzellan referenziert die Region um Swansea, in der er nach dem Ersten Weltkrieg als Klempner lebte und arbeitete. Williams Enkelin erinnert sich, wie sie Solitär spielten und ihr Grossvater sie darum bat, die Zähler für ihn zu verschieben, da er dies aufgrund der eingeschränkten Fingerfertigkeit seiner rekonstruierten Hände nicht mehr so gut selber tun konnte. Die Stunden- (Hour), Minuten- (Minutes), und Sekundenzeiger (Seconds) referenzieren stillschweigend das «HMS», was Teil des Schiffnamens der Royal Navy darstellt. Sie sind so eingestellt, dass sie als Zeichen in Gestalt des nautischen Winkalphabets den Titel des Werks abbilden – einen Satz, den der Marinegefreite Vicarage geäussert haben mag, wenn er mit seiner Enkelin während eines Spiels gesprochen hat.

EDIUM: Solitärbrett aus Porzellan, Fundstücke von Uhren
MASSE: 40 × 40 × 5 cm

JAHR: 2017

Make my move for me, will you, my Love

Imagining the work

This piece is the culmination of 15 years' research and making work about British servicemen who sustained facial injuries in World War I and underwent pioneering facial reconstructive surgery at the hands of surgical pioneer Sir Harold Gillies. The work was inspired by the story of Able Seaman William Vicarage, the first British serviceman to undergo the tubed pedicle method of skin grafting, and by Paddy Hartley's much later conversations with his granddaughter. William served in the Royal Navy on HMS Malaya as part of the 5th Battle Squadron under the command of Vice-Admiral Sir Hugh Evan-Thomas. He sustained severe cordite burns to his face and hands during the Battle of Jutland (31 May—1 June 1916).

No public record of William's experience existed prior to Paddy Hartley's getting to know his family, and tracking his family down was a major highlight of the artist's professional career. It is to be hoped that the information and insights uncovered in the course of this project will stimulate recognition of the immensely significant part played by Williams' experience in the development of facial reconstructive surgery. More can be read about Williams at http://paddyhartley.com/vicarage-1.

"Make my move for me, will you, my Love" combines a series of references to William's life story. His original trade as a watchmaker is reflected in the Solitaire counters, while the porcelain game board refers to the region of Swansea in which he lived and worked as a plumber's mate after World War I. William's granddaughter recalls how they would play board games such as Solitaire and how her grandfather would ask her to move the counters for him, being unable to do so himself as easily as he might have wished due to the reduced dexterity of his reconstructed hands.

Tacitly referencing the 'HMS' the Hour, Minute and Second hands, that forms part of the names of vessels of the British Royal Navy, are configured to display characters in semaphore code to present the title of the piece — the kind of phrase that Able Seaman Vicarage may have used when talking with his granddaughter during the course of a game.

MEDIA: Porcelain Solitaire board, horology salvage
DIMENSIONS: 40 × 40 × 5 cm

DATE: 2017

Golgotha (souvenir)

Die Konzeption des Werks

Diese Arbeit wurde als Anhang zu Paddy Hartleys Masterarbeit «Nativity» geschaffen, die ihrerseits als Reaktion auf die Entwicklung des Klonens und der ethischen Debatten um diese Technologie entwickelt wurde, besonders im Hinblick auf die Haltungen religiöser Gruppen. Golgotha ist ein unbeschwerter Beitrag zu dem Werk, konzipiert als Antwort auf die Vermarktung religiösen Glaubens.

MEDIUM: Weisses Steinzeug, weisse Zinnglasur, Perlmuttluster
MASSE: ca. 38 × 30 × 15 cm
JAHR: 1999/2000

Golgotha (souvenir)

Imagining the work

This piece was made as an appendix to Paddy Hartley's MA graduation work 'Nativity', which itself had been made in response to developments in cloning and the ethical debates around this technology, particularly regarding attitudes of religious groups. Golgotha was a light-hearted appendix to the work, responding to the merchandising of religious belief.

MEDIA: White earthenware, white tin glaze, mother of pearl lustre
DIMENSIONS: c. 38 × 30 × 15 cm

DATE: 1999/2000

Papaver Rhoeas (Poppy)

Die Konzeption des Werks

Papaver Rhoeas (Klatschmohn) sind einzigartig geschaffene Kunstwerke, die sich auf die Gedenkfeiern zum Ersten Weltkrieg und anderer Konflikte beziehen. Paddy Hartley hat diese in Zusammenarbeit mit einem herausragenden Team von Wissenschaftlern geschaffen, um zeitgenössische Auffassungen zur Andenken- und Erinnerungskultur zur Debatte zu stellen.

Die Skulpturen bestehen aus Lammherzgewebe, Pferdehaar und alten chirurgischen Nähfäden, sie sind als pathologische Präparate in eigens mundgeblasenen Glasgefässen ausgestellt, welche die Form von Patronenhülsen des Ersten Weltkriegs aufnehmen. Die Farben und Formen der Mohnblumen sind verschieden, je nach angewandter Technik. Dem Nationalitätenkult oder der Verehrung der Anzahl Gefallenen entgegengesetzt, würdigen die Papaver Rhoeas schlicht die Anzahl der Leben, die durch bewaffnete Konflikte verloren gingen, seien die Opfer Soldaten oder Zivilisten gewesen, jung oder alt oder auch von spezifischer Ethnie oder Religion. Die Papaver Rhoeas rücken unsere universelle Verwundbarkeit in den Vordergrund.

Als Ergebnis seiner intensiven Auseinandersetzung mit Gewebe in Zusammenarbeit mit Partnern aus der Wissenschaft, hat Paddy eine Anzahl dieser Skulpturen mit einer dynamischen Komponente der graduellen Zersetzung und Auflösung über ihre Lebensdauer hinweg versehen. Das physische Objekt wird sich verwandeln, um einzig als Erinnerung in den Gedächtnissen der Betrachter weiterzuexistieren. Als temporäre, vergängliche und ephemere Kunstwerke stellen die Papaver Rhoeas die Verehrung materieller Spuren der Vergangenheit in Frage und bieten stattdessen ein bedeutungsschweres, vitales und flüchtiges Erinnerungssymbol an.

Sich in permanenter Entwicklung befindend, bleiben Paddys Mohnblumen ein Spiegel für das Gedächtnis an sich und einige davon sind zudem ihrer eigenen Vergänglichkeit ausgeliefert, womit sie der künstlich erzeugten Beständigkeit des kollektiven Gedächtnisses zuwiderlaufen. Er stellt zur Debatte, dass eine lebhaftere Auseinandersetzung mit dem Gedenken die Fähigkeit zu vergessen beinhalten kann.

MEDIUM: Lammherz-Gewebe, Glas, Pferdehaar, historischer chirurgischer Baumwollfaden, Wasser
MASSE: Installation 50 × 15 × 15 cm, print 100 × 100 × 5 cm

JAHR: 2018

Papaver Rhoeas (Poppy)

Drawing on the poppy's synonymity with the commemoration of World War I and other conflicts, Papaver Rhoeas (l. Field poppy) are uniquely crafted artworks produced by Paddy Hartley in collaboration with a unique team of science practitioners that address contemporary notions of remembrance and the cultural phenomena of memorialisation.

Papaver Rhoeas sculptures are composed of lamb's heart tissue, horsehair and vintage suture cotton and are presented as pathological specimens in custom-made blown-glass vessels inspired by the forms of spent World War I artillery shells. Each poppy varies in colour and composition, based on the treatment and processing of the tissue. As opposed to drawing an affinity to nationality or numbers of dead, Papaver Rhoeas simply acknowledges lives lost during conflict whether they are service personnel or civilian, young or old, or from any faith or ethnic background. Papaver Rhoeas emphasise our universally shared vulnerability of the flesh.

As a result of intensive tissue processing in collaboration with his science partners, Paddy has created a selection of these sculptures, adding the specific dynamic of gradual fragmentation and disintegration over their own lifespan. The physical object will literally transfigure to exist solely as a memory in the mind of the viewer. As temporary, transitory and ephemeral artworks, the Papaver Rhoeas sculptures dispute the veneration of the material trace and present a charged, vital and momentary reliquary for remembrance and memory.

Paddy's poppies remain a mirror for memory itself, being in a state of permanent evolution and, in some cases, susceptible to their own mortality, counter to the preservation and artificial persistence of collective memory. He presents the notion that a more vigorous and productive interaction with remembrance may well entail an ability to forget.

MEDIA: Lamb's-heart tissue, glass, horsehair, vintage suture cotton, water
DIMENSIONS: Sculpture 50 × 15 × 15 cm, print 100 × 100 × 5 cm

DATE: 2018

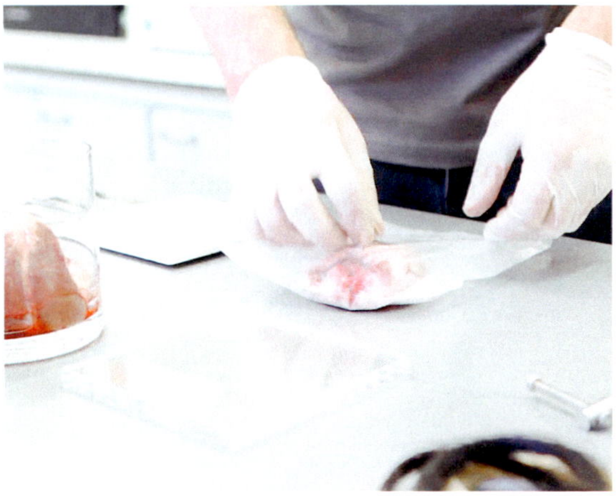
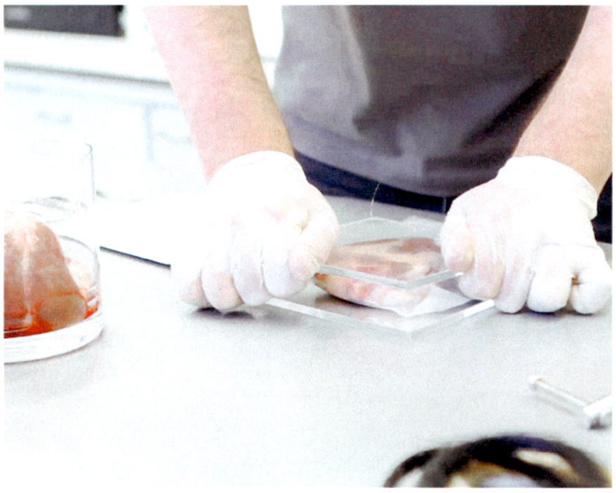
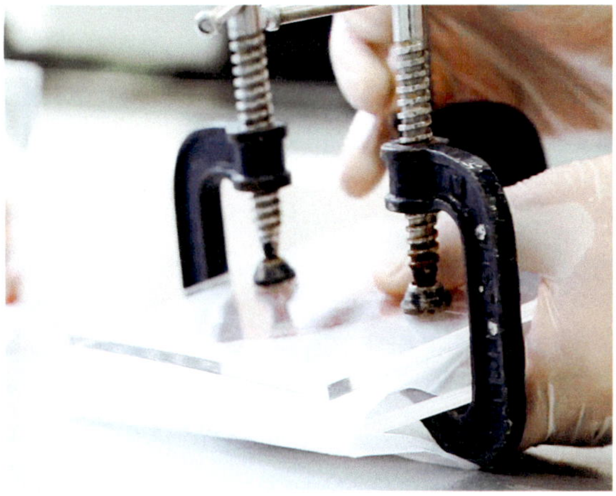
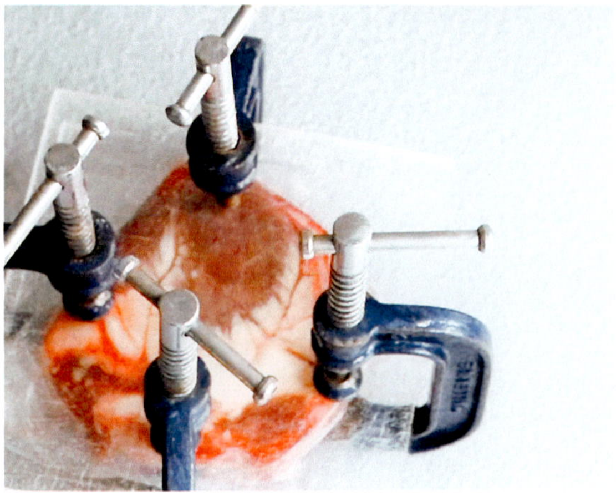

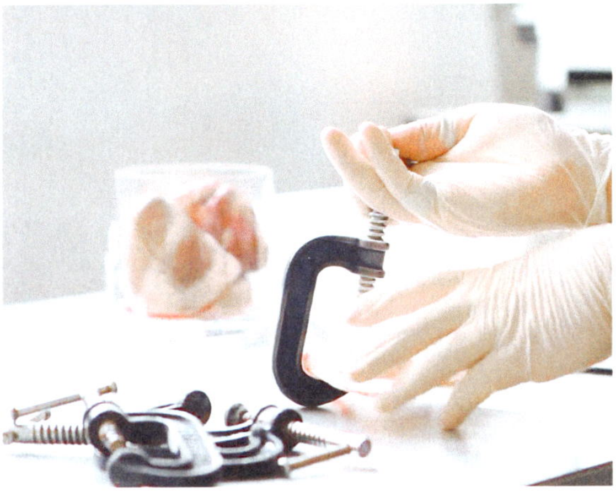
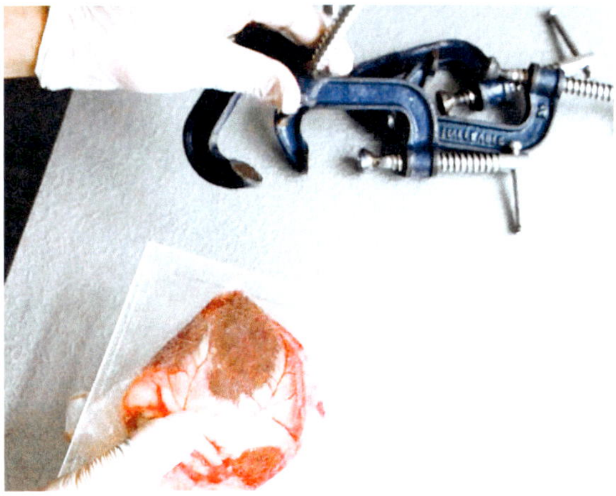

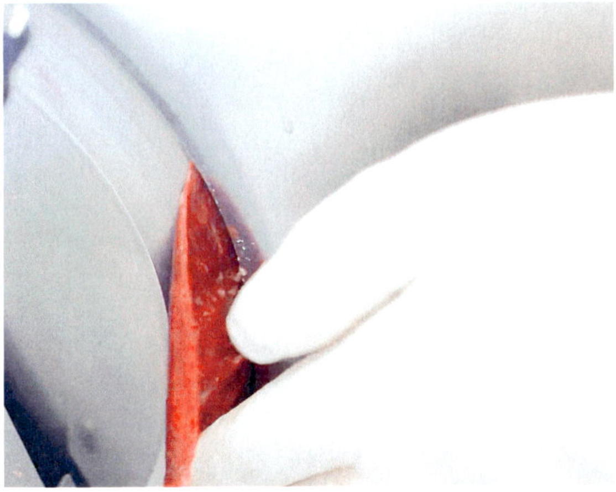

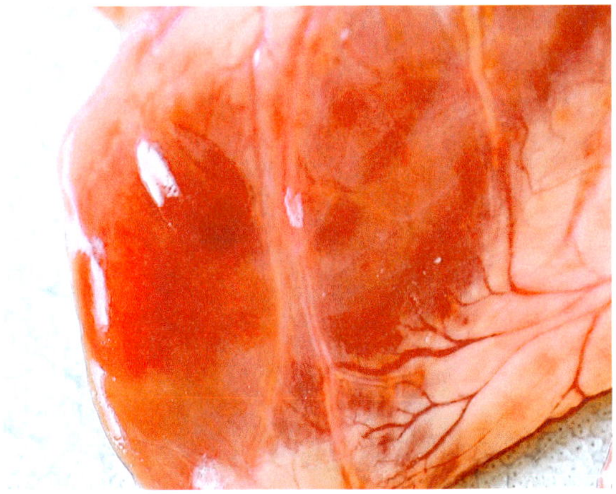

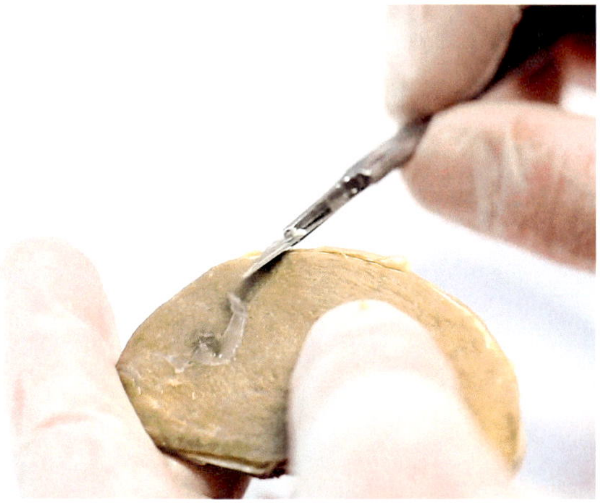

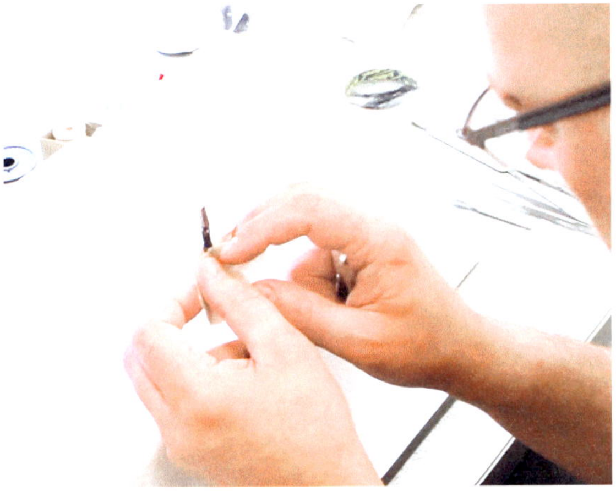

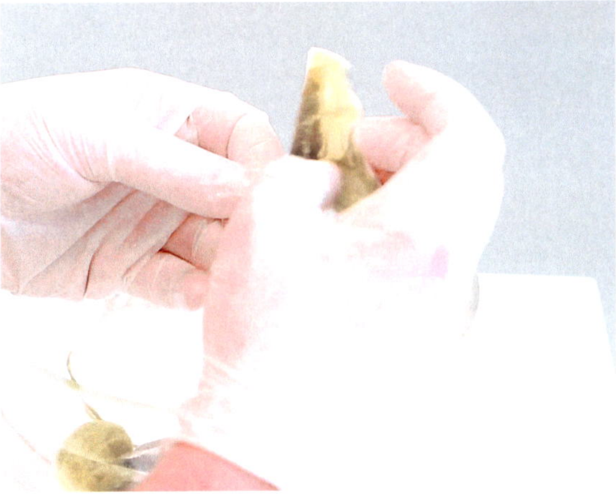
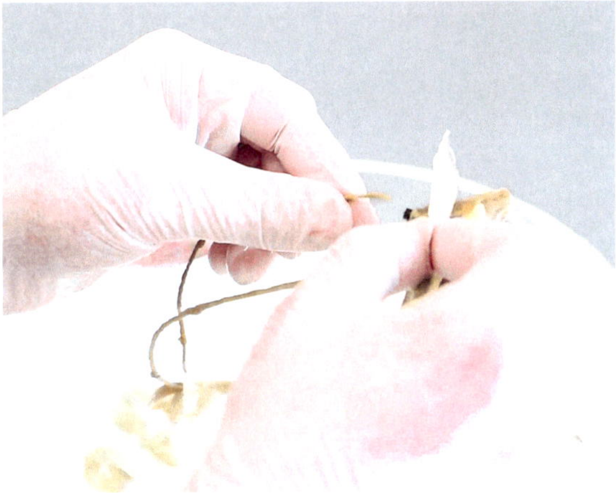
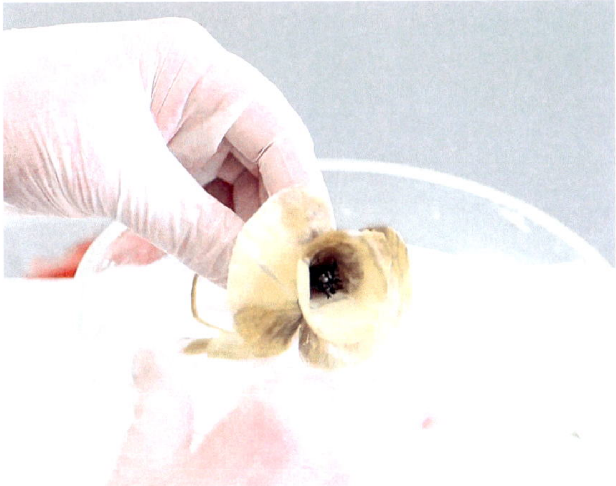

Inter— vention

Von Gestern zum
Heute und Morgen

From the past to the
present and future

Veranstaltungsort · The Venue

DAS PHARMAZIEMUSEUM der Universität Basel befindet sich im «Haus zum Sessel», das zuerst 1316 erwähnt wurde. 1507 wurde es zum Sitz des berühmtesten Druckers seiner Zeit, Johannes Frobenius. Sein Talent in der Herstellung einiger der schönsten Bücher der Epoche zog Koryphäen wie Erasmus von Rotterdam, Hans Holbein d. J. oder Theophrastus von Hohenheim, besser bekannt als Paracelsus, an. Seit 1924 ist hier das Pharmaziemuseum der Universität Basel untergebracht, eine der bedeutendsten Sammlungen zur Geschichte der Pharmazie. Sie hat als klassische akademische Sammlung überdauert, das Museum wurde sorgsam restauriert ohne den ursprünglichen Charakter zu beeinträchtigen. Als seltenes Raritätenkabinett löst das Museum sowohl bei Kunstschaffenden wie auch bei Forschern regelmässig Begeisterung aus. Im obersten Stockwerk, wo auch die Sammlung der Apothekenkeramiken untergebracht ist, hat Paddy Hartley seine geistreiche und provokative Intervention eingebracht, die aus rund 30 kleinen Porzellan-Föten besteht. Sie treiben hier in der dichtgedrängten Sammlung Unfug und überraschen die Betrachter inmitten der historischen Objekte aus der Wissenschaft der Heilkunde.

THE PHARMACY MUSEUM of the Basel University is located in the 'House zum Sessel' which first was mentioned in 1316. In 1507 it became the home and workshop of the most famous printer of his era, Johannes Frobenius. His unique skill in producing some of the most beautiful books of the time attracted luminaries like Erasmus of Rotterdam, Hans Holbein the Younger or Theophrastus of Hohenheim, better known as Paracelsus. Since 1924, the building houses the Pharmacy Museum of the University of Basel, one of the world's most important and extensive collections on the history of pharmacy. Still in its original state displaying its collections in the classic academic style, the museum has been carefully restored without compromising the original intent. As a rare cabinet of treasures it has become a favourite of artists and scientists alike. On its top floor which contains the collection of apothecary ceramics, Paddy Hartley has introduced his witty and provocative intervention in the form of roughly 30 small porcelain foetuses. They are up to mischief and surprise the viewer within the dense fabric of historic objects related to the science of maintaining good health.

Paddy Hartley spricht über seine liebsten Kunstwerke

Mit wenigen Ausnahmen bewundere ich einzelne Kunstwerke und nicht so sehr das Gesamtwerk eines Kunstschaffenden. Nach meiner Ansicht gibt es eine Qualität der «Korrektheit» eines Kunstwerks, das in sich wirklich stimmig ist: Vom Konzept über die Materialisierung, die Technik, die Ausführung bis zur Präsentation; eine Harmonie, die alles zusammen korrekt und stimmig erscheinen lässt. In diesen Fällen finde ich es eine ziemliche Herausforderung, darüber zu sprechen, weil das Werk an sich genau ausdrückt, was es soll.

Jeder künstlerische Zugang ist meiner Meinung nach gültig, weil Künstler sehr unterschiedliche Arten der Kommunikation haben und die Betrachter ihre eigene Interpretation einbringen, die auf der jeweiligen Lebenserfahrung beruht. Jedes Kunstwerk, das jemals geschaffen wurde, kommuniziert etwas, ist mit jemandem verbunden und bedeutet etwas für jemanden, sei es die Person, die es geschaffen hat oder der Betrachter. Diese Qualität der absoluten Korrektheit ist sehr selten und aussergewöhnlich, auch die Wahrnehmung, was diese ausmacht, verändert sich von einer Person zur nächsten. Sollte ich je ein Werk schaffen, das von auch nur einem Menschen als solches Werk wahrgenommen wird — nun ja, das wäre an sich unvergleichlich.

Hier folgt eine Liste einiger meiner liebsten Kunstwerke:

Fiona Banner: Harrier, 2010
MEDIUM: BAe Sea Harrier Flugzeug, Farbe

Cristóvão Canhavato (Kester): Throne of Weapons, 2002
MEDIUM: Ausgemusterte Automatikwaffen

Jake and Dinos Chapman: Fucking Hell, 2008 (eine Neuschöpfung von Jake und Dinos Chapmans «Hell», welches 1999 durch ein Feuer zerstört wurde)
MEDIUM: Eine Installation bestehend aus Glasvitrinen mit 8cm hohen Figuren

Matt Collishaw: Throbbing Gristle, 2008
MEDIUM: Aluminium, Motor, Gips, Kunstharz, Stahl, Stroboskop-Leuchten

Marcel Duchamp: Nude Descending a Staircase, No. 2, 1912
MEDIUM: Öl auf Leinwand

Jacob Epstein: Rock Drill, 1913–15
MEDIUM: Bronze

Richard Notkin: Satirical teapots
MEDIUM: Steinzeug
Alle Teekannen von Richard Notkin sind technisch verblüffend, regen zum Denken an und sind voll fabelhaften Humors.

George E. Ohr: Ceramics
Der selbsternannte «Verrückte Töpfer von Biloxi», er war seiner Zeit um Jahrzehnte voraus.

Cornelia Parker: Cold Dark Matter, 1991
MEDIUM: Explodiertes Gartenhaus — Holz, Metall, Kunststoff, Keramik, Papier, Textilien und Draht

Marc Quinn: SELF, 1991
MEDIUM: Eigenes Blut, Edelstahl, Plexiglas und Kühlaggregat

Geoffrey Swindell: Ceramics
Alles meines früheren Lehrers ist erstaunlich und weist einen wundervollen Sinn für Humor auf.

Yves Tanguy: The Invisibles, 1951
MEDIUM: Öl auf Leinwand

Bill Woodrow: Car Door, Armchair and Incident, 1981
MEDIUM: Autotür, Lehnstuhl und Emailfarbe

Takeshi Yasuda: Ceramics
Die Steinzeug-Objekte des Keramikers Takeshi Yasuda sind atemberaubend.

Paddy Hartley on his Favourite Artworks

With a few exceptions, I'm an admirer of individual artworks rather than the entire body of work created by an artist. To my mind, there is a quality of 'correctness' to any piece of art that really works. I look for every element in the piece, from concept through material, technique and execution to presentation, to be so completely in harmony that everything just feels correct. In such cases, I find it quite challenging to talk about the piece because it communicates exactly what it needs to.

In my opinion, all artistic approaches are valid because artists have very different ways of communicating, and every viewer will bring their own interpretation to the piece, based on their own life experience. Every artwork that has ever been made has communicated something, connected with someone and meant something to someone, whether the maker or the viewer. That quality of absolute correctness is a rare and sublime thing, and perceptions of what constitutes it will vary from one individual to another. If I ever make something that even one person perceives as having that same correctness — well, that would be sublime in itself.

The following is a list of some of my favourite artworks:

Fiona Banner: ***Harrier,*** **2010**
MEDIA: BAe Sea Harrier aircraft, paint

Cristóvão Canhavato (Kester): ***Throne of Weapons,*** **2002**
MEDIA: Decommissioned automatic weapons

Jake and Dinos Chapman: ***Fucking Hell,*** **2008** (a recreation of Jake and Dinos Chapman's *Hell*, which was lost in a fire in 1999)
MEDIA: Installation: glass cabinets containing 2-inch figures

Matt Collishaw: ***Throbbing Gristle,*** **2008**
MATERIALS: Aluminium, motor, plaster, resin, steel, stroboscopic lights

Marcel Duchamp: ***Nude Descending a Staircase, No. 2,*** **1912**
MEDIA: Oil on canvas

Jacob Epstein: ***Rock Drill,*** **1913–15**
MEDIA: Bronze sculpture

Richard Notkin: Satirical teapots
MEDIA: Clay
Any of Richard Notkin's teapots are technically astounding, thought-provoking and full of fabulous humour.

George E. Ohr: Ceramics
The self-proclaimed "Mad Potter of Biloxi", decades ahead of his time.

Cornelia Parker: ***Cold Dark Matter,*** **1991**
MEDIA: Exploded garden shed — wood, metal, plastic, ceramic, paper, textile and wire

Marc Quinn: ***Self,*** **1991**
MEDIA: Blood (artist's), stainless steel, Perspex and refrigeration equipment

Geoffrey Swindell: Ceramics
Anything by my former tutor is stunning, and has a lovely sense of fun.

Yves Tanguy: ***The Invisibles,*** **1951**
MEDIA: Oil on canvas

Bill Woodrow: ***Car Door, Armchair and Incident,*** **1981**
MEDIA: Car door, armchair and enamel paint

Takeshi Yasuda: Ceramics
Clay objects from the hands of ceramicist Takeshi are breathtaking.

Paddy Hartleys «Cost of Life» Playlist

Alle Kunstwerke in «The Cost of Life» wurden zu einem besonderen Soundtrack geschaffen. Paddy Hartley erläutert, was er während der Arbeit im Studio gehört hat und was diese Lieder für ihn bedeuten.

The playlist:

The End... to be continued (Urnen)
TITEL: *Fly on the Windscreen (Final)*
KÜNSTLER: Depeche Mode
AUFNAHMEJAHR: 1986
Das fünfte Album von Depeche Mode, Black Celebration, ist seit 30 Jahren eine meiner meist geliebten Aufnahmen. Dieser Titel, mit seiner ersten Zeile «Death is everywhere», ist mein besonderes Lieblingsstück, das ich im Studio dauernd höre. Viele der Lieder auf diesem Album beeindrucken mich und dies war besonders während des Jahres, in dem ich an «Cost of Life» gearbeitet habe, der Fall, in dem ich auch mein Zuhause und mein Studio nach Berwick-upon-Tweed umgezogen habe. Jeder Song auf «Black Celebration» fühlt sich sorgfältig zusammengestellt an: Alles ist an seinem richtigen Platz und gleichzeitig poetisch, melancholisch, sanftmütig, wütend und leidenschaftlich. Es ist der Höhepunkt der elektronischen Musik.

Ill Communication (Schüsseln)
TITEL: *Aquarius / Let the Sunshine in (the Flesh Failures)*
KÜNSTLER: The 5th Dimension
AUFNAHMEJAHR: 1969
Während des Winters 2020-21 arbeitete ich in meinem Studio bei Eiseskälte, wobei mir die Freude und positive Grundstimmung dieses Lieds und besonders des live-Fernsehauftritts der Gruppe The 5th Dimension von 1970, als perfektes Gegenmittel zu der Kälte — und auch zu der herausfordernden Arbeit an den empfindlichen Werkstücken — diente.

Looking Class (Spiegel)
TITEL: *I Only Have Eyes for You*
KÜNSTLER: The Flamingos
Aufnahmejahr: 1959
Dieses Lied, das im Text und der Instrumentierung eine verschrobene Liebe ausdrückt, spielte ich während der Arbeit an Spiegel immer wieder ab und es nahm eine beinahe hypnotische Qualität für mich an, für immer in sich selbst verloren. Es ist wahnsinnig schön und gleichzeitig beunruhigend, verstörend und auch gestört.

HypoTrypanoPharmAlethephobia or: The Frustration of the Virologist (Hydra)
TITEL: *I Don't Need No Doctor*
KÜNSTLER: W.A.S.P.
AUFNAHMEJAHR: 1987
Seit meinen späten Teenagerjahren ist dieses Lied einer meiner Favoriten. Manche mögen die Versionen von Ray Charles oder John Mayer überlegen finden, aber meine Wahl fällt auf die Version, die von Humble Pie live auf dem L.A. Forum 1973 aufgenommen wurde. Sie wird nur von dieser durch W.A.S.P. 1987 aufgenommenen Version übertroffen, vor allem dank des verrückten, kreischenden Gesangs von Blackie Lawless.

You Can Have Any Colour As Long as it's Blue (Roulette-Kessel)
TITEL: *Your Molecular Structure*
KÜNSTLER: Mose Allison
AUFNAHMEJAHR: 1968
Die Roulette-Kessel von «The Cost of Life» waren technisch äusserst anspruchsvoll herzustellen und ich benötigte Ruhe und Bestärkung, um die wochenlange Arbeit daran zu Ende zu führen. Mose Allison hat mich die ganze Zeit über begleitet und als ich die Teile zu einer Einheit zusammenführte, lief dieser Titel kontinuierlich.

The Infinity Balance (Waage)
TITEL: *Theme for Great Cities*
KÜNSTLER: Simple Minds
AUFNAHMEJAHR: 1981
Durch die sich wiederholende Struktur von Theme for Great Cities ist dies ein grossartiges Lied, um dazu zu arbeiten. Es drängt sich nicht ins Bewusstsein wenn ich mich auf eine Arbeit konzentriere, aber ich höre ihm zu. Anfang und Ende sind gleich, unendlich zyklisch: Theoretisch könnte es eine unendliche Schleife bilden und oftmals, wenn ich diesem Stück zuhöre, fällt mir nicht einmal auf, dass es leiser wird und von neuem beginnt.

Paddy Hartley's 'Cost of Life' Playlist

All of the artworks in 'The Cost of Life' suite were built to a specific soundtrack. Paddy Hartley recounts what he was listening to in his studio as he worked, and what those songs mean to him.

The playlist:

The End... to be continued (Urns)
TRACK: ***Fly on the Windscreen (Final)***
ARTIST(S): Depeche Mode
YEAR OF RECORDING: 1986
Depeche Mode's fifth album *Black Celebration* has been one of my most-loved records for well over 30 years. This track, with its opening line "Death is everywhere", is a particular favourite of mine and is a constant in the studio. So many songs on this album have a resonance for me, and this was especially the case while I was working on the year-long 'Cost of Life' commission and relocating my home and studio to Berwick-upon-Tweed. Each song on *Black Celebration* feels 'assembled': everything is there for a reason and is at one and the same time poetic, melancholy, tender, angry and passionate. The peak of electronic music.

Ill Communication (Dishes)
TRACK: ***Aquarius / Let the Sunshine in (the Flesh Failures)***
ARTIST(S): The 5th Dimension
YEAR OF RECORDING: 1969
Working in bracingly cold conditions in my studio during the winter of 2020–21, the joy and positivity in this song, and especially the 5th Dimension's live TV performance of it from 1970, were the perfect antidote to the cold — and also to the delicate and challenging nature of the build.

Looking Class (Mirror)
TRACK: ***I Only Have Eyes for You***
ARTIST(S): The Flamingos
Year of recording: 1959
The warped love expressed in both the lyric and the instrumentation of this track, which I played on repeat while working on The Mirror, became almost hypnotic to me, endlessly lost within itself. It is insanely beautiful and at the same time uneasy, disturbing and, indeed, deranged.

***HypoTrypanoPharmAlethephobia* or: The Frustration of the Virologist (Hydra)**
TRACK: ***I Don't Need No Doctor***
ARTIST(S): W.A.S.P.
YEAR OF RECORDING: 1987
This song has been a favourite of mine since my late teens. Some may consider the versions by Ray Charles or John Mayer superior, but my preference is for the live version recorded by Humble Pie at the L.A. Forum in 1973, trumped only by this 1987 version by W.A.S.P., with its demented, screeching vocals by Blackie Lawless.

You Can Have Any Colour As Long as it's Blue (Roulette Wheel)
TRACK: ***Your Molecular Structure***
ARTIST(S): Mose Allison
YEAR OF RECORDING: 1968
The roulette wheels in 'The Cost of Life' were a technically challenging build, and I needed calm reassurance for the weeks of work required to complete this make. Mose Allison accompanied me all the way, and when the build started to come together, this track was pretty much on repeat.

The Infinity Balance (Scales)
TRACK: ***Theme for Great Cities***
ARTIST(S): Simple Minds
YEAR OF RECORDING: 1981
The nature of the repeating structure of *Theme for Great Cities* makes it a fabulous tune to work along to. It doesn't intrude on my mind when I'm focusing on a task, but I still hear it and listen. Its beginning and end are the same, endlessly cyclical: in theory, it could be an endless loop, and often when I listen to this piece, I don't even hear it fade out and back in again.

Cambridge

Basel

Berwick

Riga

Jelgava

Texte von
Jonathan Steffen

Übersetzungen
und Herausgeber
Alexander Lukas Bieri

Fotografien
Basile Bornand

Alle anderen
Fotografien
Paddy Hartley

Gestaltung
Alexey Murashko

Druck
Jelgavas tipogrāfija

Dieses Buch wurde in der Bradford LL von Laurenz Brunner (Zürich), Gerbera von Gayaneh Bagdasaryan (Berlin) und Vjacheslav Kirilenko (Almaty) gesetzt.

HAUT. *Stratum corneum*: Constellation Snow Country & Lime 350 g/m^2 von Fedrigoni (Verona). *Epidermis*: Colorit Red 38 160 g/m^2 von Lessebo Paper (Lessebo). *Dermis*: Munken Polar Board 960 g/m^2 von Arctic Paper (Munkedals). *Hypodermis*: Splendorgel EW 115 g/m^2 von Fedrigoni. FLEISCH: Splendorgel EW 115 g/m^2 von Fedrigoni. KNOCHEN: Arctic Volume Ice 130 g/m^2 von Arctic Paper.

Texts by
Jonathan Steffen

Translator
and publisher
Alexander Lukas Bieri

Photography by
Basile Bornand

Additional
photography by
Paddy Hartley

Design
Alexey Murashko

Print
Jelgavas tipogrāfija

The edition is set in Bradford LL by Laurenz Brunner (Zürich), Gerbera by Gayaneh Bagdasaryan (Berlin) and Vyacheslav Kirilenko (Almaty).

SKIN. *Stratum corneum*: Constellation Snow Country & Lime 350 gsm by Fedrigoni (Verona). *Epidermis*: Colorit Red 38 160 gsm by Lessebo Paper (Lessebo). *Dermis*: Munken Polar Board 960 gsm by Arctic Paper (Munkedals). *Hypodermis*: Splendorgel EW 115 gsm by Fedrigoni. FLESH: Splendorgel EW 115 gsm by Fedrigoni. BONES: Arctic Volume Ice 130 gsm by Arctic Paper.

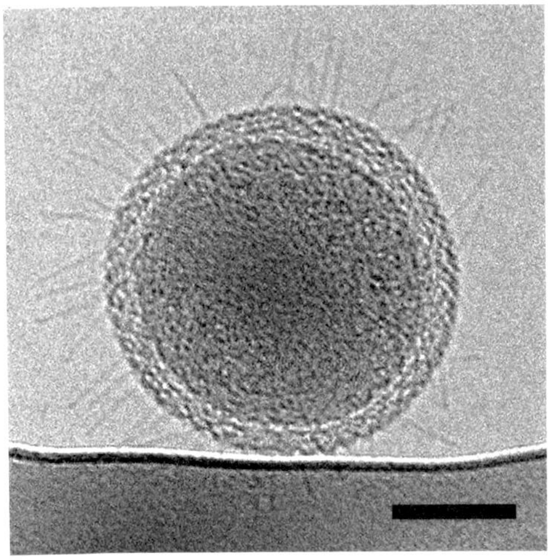

IM JAHR 2015 ENTDECKTEN DIE FORSCHER des Berkeley Lab mittels Kryo-Elektronentomographie im Grundwasser ultrakleine Bakterien, die noch nie zuvor gesehen worden waren. Der Massstabsbalken misst 100 Nanometer (Bildnachweis: Berkeley Lab). Die Cover-Komposition und das Raster dieses Buches orientieren sich an der Form und dem Massstabsverhältnis dieser Zellen an der unteren Grössengrenze des Lebens.

IN 2015, THE RESEARCHERS of the Berkeley Lab — using cryo-electron tomography — discovered in groundwater ultra-small bacterias never seen before. The scale bar is 100 nanometers (image courtesy: Berkeley Lab). The cover composition and the grid of this book draws on the form and the scale ratio of these cells found at the lower size limit of life.

BILDNACHWEISE. Fotografien Seiten 8–17 — Historisches Archiv Roche. Foto Seite 65 von Stefan Schmidlin. Filmstills Seiten 168–171 von Raquel Couceiro and Tod Ivanov.

IMAGE CREDITS. Photographs pp. 8–17 — The Roche Historical Collection & Archive. Photograph p. 65 by Stefan Schmidlin. Film stills pp. 168–171 by Raquel Couceiro and Tod Ivanov.

ISBN 978-3-9525350-1-1